Make and Do

Helping young children discover God,
through art and craft

MAKE AND DO
© Scripture Union 2007
First published 2007
ISBN 978 184427 272 3

Scripture Union, 207-209 Queensway, Bletchley,
Milton Keynes, MK2 2EB, England
Email: info@scriptureunion.org.uk
Website: www.scriptureunion.org.uk

Scripture Union Australia
Locked Bag 2, Central Coast Business Centre, NSW 2252
Website: www.scriptureunion.org.au

Scripture Union USA
PO Box 987, Valley Forge, PA 19482
Website: www.scriptureunion.org

Scripture quotations are from the Contemporary English Version
© American Bible Society 1991, 1992, 1995.
Anglicisations © British and Foreign Bible Society 1997,
published in the UK by HarperCollinsPublishers. Used by permission.

British Library Cataloguing-in-Publication Data.
A catalogue record of this book is available from the British Library.

Printed and bound in China by 1010 Printing International Limited

Cover design: Mark Carpenter Design Consultants

Tiddly characters created by Mark Carpenter

Internal design: Mark Carpenter Design Consultants

Photography: Steve Shipman, David Vary

Tiddlywinks series editor: Maggie Barfield

Writers: Maggie Barfield, Kathleen Crawford, Marjory Francis,
Val Mullally, Priscilla Trood

Illustration: Victoria Barfield www.galleryvictoria.co.uk

Illustrator's assistant: Joshua Barfield

Scripture Union is an international Christian charity working with churches in
more than 130 countries, providing resources to bring the good news about
Jesus Christ to children, young people and families and to encourage them to
develop spiritually through the Bible and prayer.
As well as our network of volunteers, staff and associates who run holidays,
church-based events and school Christian groups, we produce a wide range of
publications and support those who use our resources through training
programmes.

What's inside Make and Do?

The how and why of Make and Do

'Art and craft activities can be messy, time-consuming and expensive – so, are they really worth all the effort?' asks a children's group leader.

The answer is, not surprisingly in a book of art and craft activities, 'Yes!'

Art and craft activities give young children opportunities to express themselves, build confidence and skills, solve problems and explore and express their emotions. But most importantly, these are ways in which children are able to meet with God and discover the truths of the Bible. And that's what *Tiddlywinks: Make and Do* is all about.

Does that sound too ambitious? Well, it *is* ambitious because we are accepting a momentous and God-given task when we start to ask, 'How can children meet God?' One way is through art and craft. Exploring creativity and developing skills are means

for children to grow in confidence, nurture a sense of belonging, and stimulate a sense of worth. Each of these factors has spiritual significance and can help the youngest child (and the oldest adult!) grow in their own faith and relationship with God.

Along the way, there will be a whole lot of fun, a guaranteed amount of mess and clearing-up, wonderful masterpieces and spectacular disasters. And through making, chatting, helping, wondering, attempting and exploring, there will be something amazing happening as each of us discovers more about who God is, what he is like, what he says and does and how we can be his friends. What are you waiting for?!

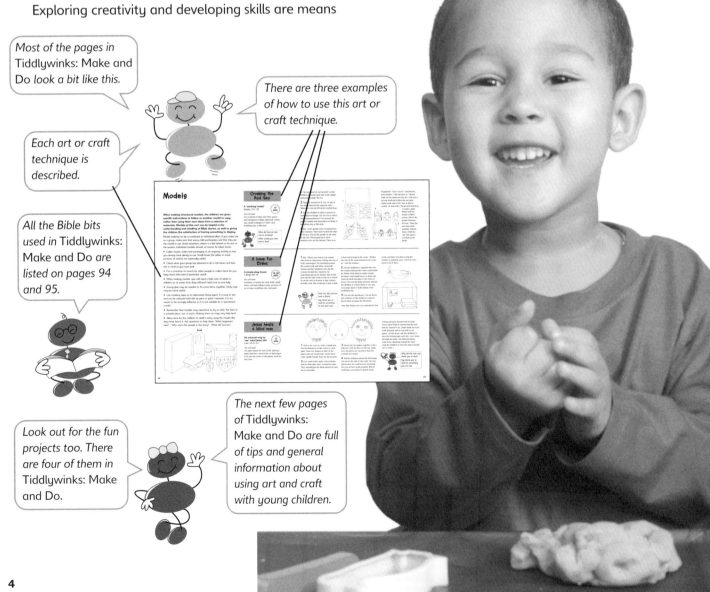

Most of the pages in Tiddlywinks: Make and Do *look a bit like this.*

There are three examples of how to use this art or craft technique.

Each art or craft technique is described.

All the Bible bits used in Tiddlywinks: Make and Do *are listed on pages 94 and 95.*

Look out for the fun projects too. There are four of them in Tiddlywinks: Make and Do.

The next few pages of Tiddlywinks: Make and Do *are full of tips and general information about using art and craft with young children.*

Basics

Art and craft activities are not only about 'keeping children busy' but about nurturing children's self-esteem, creativity, spirituality and personal relationship with Jesus. This page will help you know where to start. It is important to prepare beforehand and have the materials and equipment ready.

Organising

How you organise your craft area will depend very much on the facilities you have available.

Some basic principles to follow:

● If there are other activities going on in the room, make your craft area at one end of the room, not in the middle.

● If you have a washbasin in the room, set up the craft table near this.

● You will need a table for the children to sit or stand at, to carry out the activity.

● Only allow a small number of children round the table at one time. Repeat the activity with another small group rather than crowding.

● Ideally, keep materials on a separate surface nearby. Use open containers and place them at the children's eye level, so that they can help themselves as they need them (fabric, coloured papers, glue sticks).

● Have a space available to put the completed work to dry. An art rack can be expensive but is very helpful. Perhaps you could use a washing line and pegs.

● Site your craft table where the floor can be brushed or washed easily.

Equipment

● If possible, keep your equipment and materials in clearly labelled containers in a cupboard nearby. Otherwise use stacking plastic boxes which are easily transported.

● If funding is limited, think carefully about your shopping list. Consider linking up with other groups and buying in bulk. If another group uses the same premises, perhaps you can share resources (which is a help financially and where there is limited storage space).

● Table covers can be made from PVC-covered cloth (from fabric shops). You will need a separate one for food preparation. Use disposable plastic sheeting when working with clay: it is easier to throw it away than to try and clean up.

● Spread floor covers flat to avoid tripping, and secure the edges with masking tape. Ideally, get everyone to wear shoes with grip, like trainers.

● Use white glue when materials are difficult to secure. It works well and is cost-effective, especially when bought in bulk from a DIY shop. Glue sticks are easy for little hands to handle and reduce the mess considerably. Check that all glue is non-toxic, and suitable for your age group.

● Use quality round-ended safety scissors that cut well. There is nothing more frustrating than scissors that will not cut. Also have a couple of pairs of left-handed scissors. Supervise all use of scissors closely. Children from two-and-a-half years upwards, with adequate co-ordination, can be guided to use scissors effectively.

● Use suitable washable poster paint. Provide white plus primary colours, (red, yellow and blue), which can be used to make other colours: red and yellow make orange; red and blue make purple; blue and yellow make green. A large bottle of each will last a long time. Paint brushes need to be short and chunky.

● It is much easier and less messy for children to paint at an easel but a covered table is fine.

● Plastic aprons, with long cuffed sleeves are ideal for children this age. Otherwise, old shirts make a good alternative (not too big). Put the shirt on backwards and button up. Do up the cuffs and turn them up to the required length.

● Non-spill paint pots are inexpensive and can be found at many craft or toy shops.

● Lining paper is good for painting. Cut lengths in advance and lay them under books to flatten. Sugar paper has various uses and is cheap and colourful. Small hands need big paper so provide a minimum size of A4 sheets. If possible buy card in bulk from stationery catalogues, or office stores. Find out if you have a paper factory or recycling centre in your area that you could use. Tissue paper and crêpe paper are reasonably inexpensive and very useful.

● Collect collage materials to use in the sessions: scraps of yarn and fabric; sweet wrappers and foil cake cups; pasta shapes; wrapping paper; magazines; cereal boxes; large pieces of cardboard; egg boxes; yogurt pots; the inside of kitchen rolls. Most things can be of use.

Supplies

Must haves

plain white paper
coloured paper
white and coloured card
sugar paper (or large backing paper)
lining paper (long lengths)
crêpe paper
wallpaper
chunky wax crayons
broad colouring pencils (but not for very young children)
pencils
safety scissors (right and left handed)
glue sticks
'white' or 'school' glue and spreaders
ready-mixed paint (suitable for children)
broad paint brushes with short handles
sponges
shallow plastic trays
old newspapers (remove any unsuitable pictures)
cereal packets
cardboard tubes
large packaging boxes
yogurt pots
egg boxes
magazines with suitable pictures
old greetings cards

Leader's (adult) craft kit

a craft knife (optional but very useful)
sharp scissors (kept out of reach of children)
Blu-tack
sticky tape and a dispenser
paper masking tape
a hole punch
a ruler
labels
kitchen roll
wet wipes
tissues
a stapler and staples
a staple remover
a thick marker pen
coloured gel pens
paper fasteners
paper clips
string
a paper crimper (a tool to crimp paper)
plastic spoons (for stirring or ladling paint or glue)
paper towels for drying hands

Specials

glitter pens
glitter
tinsel
lametta strands
chenille wires (pipe cleaners)
sequinned fabric scraps
metallic card
metallic foil
tissue paper
embossed wallpaper
gift wrapping paper
stickers
joggle eyes (self-adhesive)
pinking or curved scissors
felt-tip pens
white and coloured chalk
stampers and ink pads
wooden spoons
short plant sticks
short flat wooden sticks (lollipop sticks)
cotton wool
natural materials (leaves, feathers, cones, twigs)
dried pasta shapes
string and knitting wool
fabric scraps
ribbon
large buttons
empty cotton reels
coloured matchsticks

Try to ensure that you always have the items in the 'Must haves' list opposite, then check the specific activity for any extra items you will need to do it. Try to 'have a place for everything and everything in its place'. Like a well-organised kitchen, the activity is far more enjoyable when you have good quality equipment and consumables, and everything is stored neatly and logically.

It is a good idea to have pictures or photographs showing the contents of each container, so that children can help with packing up.

Make sure you have regular clean-ups to discard broken odds and ends, and to check what restocking is needed.

Look out for suitable materials and equipment at pound shops or scrap stores. (Check in the telephone directory or online to find if there is a store near you.) Materials can often be found at a fraction of the usual retail price. But do be careful not to make false savings: scissors need to last long and be durable; crayons and paints need to have good quality colour and 'lay' easily onto the paper; cheap paper will wrinkle or tear when wet. Ask members of your church for materials, but make sure you make your requests specific. Always be aware of any safety or health hazards (see page 7).

Sense and safety

Craft activities are fun, but there are some basic safety issues that you will need to consider.

Make sure that:

• there are sufficient adults to supervise an activity. One adult to every four children is usually adequate. You will, however, need extra help if you are using glitter or metal confetti, to prevent it going everywhere. You will also need additional help to ensure safety if you go outdoors, for instance, to collect leaves for printing, or to rub bark and concrete. If you do not have enough leaders, ask a parent to help or postpone the activity for another time.

• protective clothing is available for the children, preferably waterproof painting overalls or aprons. Old shirts with the sleeves rolled up are a cheap alternative.

• work surfaces, and the floor underneath the working area, are protected with plastic sheeting or newspaper. Non-spill paint containers are also a good investment.

• all glue, paint, crayons, felt-tip pens and ink stamp pads provided are non-toxic and labelled as suitable for young children to use.

• the scissors provided are child safe. They should be made mainly of plastic and have rounded ends. Get them from educational suppliers and toy shops. Four-year-olds may be sufficiently confident, with supervision, to use patterned scissors. These are rounded at the ends and will make a decorative edge on paper, but the blades are not particularly sharp. Give the children opportunities to use scissors and practise cutting skills, but they will need close supervision and to be taught how to use tools safely.

• a supply of cloths is available for cleaning up after activities. Keep dishcloths which are used in the kitchen for cleaning food preparation areas or refreshment tables completely separate for hygiene reasons.

• any spillages are wiped up immediately – especially if the mess is on the floor, otherwise, someone could easily slip and injure themselves.

• you follow the instructions on the container carefully when, for example, paint gets on clothing. Most paints for use by children are washable but the stain usually needs to be treated immediately with cold water, not hot.

• you do not use polystyrene that crumbles or cardboard tubes from toilet rolls for junk modelling.

• extra care is taken when using dried peas, seeds or pulses for collage or making musical instruments. Some children will put small objects up their nose or in their ears, or could choke by trying to eat them. Make sure all home-made musical instruments, such as shakers, are securely sealed before they are used. Avoid using dried red kidney beans (which are poisonous until they have been cooked thoroughly) or any other poisonous seeds and leaves in craft work.

• pen tops are looked after by an adult, while the children are using the pens, to prevent children choking on them.

Food activities

Young children enjoy cookery and sampling the results. But:

• Make sure everyone washes their hands properly before they start the activity, and that all surfaces and utensils are thoroughly cleaned.

• Do not allow children near the oven, microwave or sharp knives, or let them touch hot items, such as a bowl of melted chocolate. Insist that they wait until the cooked food has cooled sufficiently before they taste it.

• Some children are allergic to certain food items. Check with parents or carers before you give any of these to a child. Make sure you keep a record of each child's allergies and update them regularly. If you are in doubt, put the food in bags to be eaten later. Hand it to the parents to take home.

And finally, a few reminders of general sense and safety issues.

Make sure that:

• if an accident does happen, you know where the First Aid box is located and that it is kept well stocked.

• if you are not trained in First Aid, you know someone who can help in an emergency.

• furniture is checked regularly for splinters, and toys for damage and cleanliness.

• your premises are secure. Consider having the door handle high up so only adults can open the door to go out of your room.

All UK churches now have specific guidelines for safeguarding children.

These include:

• All adult leaders and helpers who work in children's groups must be checked by the Criminal Records Bureau.

• There must also be at least two leaders in a group.

Check with the Churches' Child Protection Advisory Service or your denominational head office for the latest information.

Books

Making books is an ideal shared activity with a group of children. Each child can contribute a whole or part of a page. The finished book can be 'read' at the time, displayed for others to see, and enjoyed together again at a later date.

- Zigzag books are the easiest to make and use. Pages can be completed separately, and then hinged with sticky tape down both sides. If the pages are laminated first, the book will be particularly robust and stand up on its own.

- For a book that opens in the conventional way, pages can again be made individually. The children can help to put the pages in order. Make holes down the left-hand side and tie together loosely with ribbon or yarn.

- Children enjoy making individual books to follow through a topic. Fold three or four sheets of strong paper together and sew down the fold. Follow a topic such as 'God made me' (my eyes, ears, hands and so on) or 'The world God made' (Creation). Work on one page for each session and let the children take their books home at the end of the topic. This works best when children attend regularly.

- Write very few words in books for under 5s. Normally one or two words per page is plenty. Talking together about the topic or story is more important. Use a picture book to encourage 'Thank you' prayers or 'Please help...'

- Make pictures more interesting with collage materials and different textures, but do not make the pages too bulky.

- Make sure glue and paint are dry before putting the pages together.

- Glue extra pieces of paper along one edge to make 'lift the flaps' – it is great fun discovering what is underneath!

God makes the sun

A zigzag book
Psalm 19

15 mins

You will need:
A4 sheets of card (in blue, yellow and orange), card circles 10 cm in diameter for each child; yellow, orange and gold crayons; paint; scraps of shiny materials (paper or fabric); glue

At Peter's house

A book with pages
Mark 1:29–34

15–20 mins

You will need:
seven sheets of A3 or A4 card, collage scraps, a hole punch, knitting wool

Josiah and God's book

Making a scroll
2 Kings 22:1 – 23:3

15 mins

You will need:
sheets of A4 paper or a roll of drawing paper, sticky tape, four 25 cm lengths of dowelling or smooth bamboo cane

1 Ask the children: 'Where is the sun? What is it like? How does the sun help us?' Explain that the sun gives us light and warmth. Creatures and plants need the sun to grow.

2 Ask: 'When can't we see the sun?' Say that at night, when it is dark, the earth has turned so that the sun is facing other countries. To us, the sun seems to travel across the sky each day, rising in the morning and setting at night. (*Draw an arc in the air with your hands.*)

3 Say that God made the sun. His beautiful sky shows how great God is. Someone long ago wrote a poem about it. Read Psalm 19:1,4b–6a.

4 Give out the card circles and yellow or shiny materials. Encourage the children to decorate their sun.

5 Arrange the suns on the card, one per sheet, at varying heights to show the journey of the sun through the day. Use the orange and yellow card for the rising and setting and the blue for the rest of the day. Glue the suns down and tape the pages together in order.

6 Stand the book in a zigzag formation as you listen to the Bible verses again.

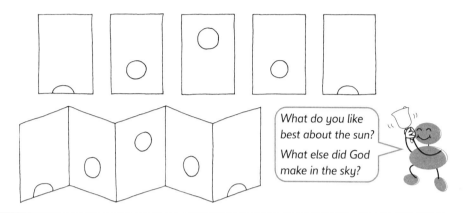

What do you like best about the sun?

What else did God make in the sky?

---

1 Tell the story briefly: 'Jesus and his friends went to Peter's house. Granny was ill in bed. Jesus helped her up and she was better straightaway! She gave everyone a meal. That evening many ill people came to see Jesus. Jesus made everyone well.'

2 Tell the children you are going to make a book about the story, together. Draw a simple picture of Jesus on a sheet of card, cut it out and punch a hole at the top. (There is a picture of Jesus to copy or trace on page 80). Say that this figure will be used on every page so the children do not need to draw Jesus in their pictures.

3 Set the children to work on their six cards, drawing and using collage to make the scenes from the story sentences in paragraph 1.

4 Use the last sheet of card to make a front cover for the book. Draw or collage a white New Testament-style house on this cover, with a dark doorway and window. Write the book title: 'Jesus at Peter's house'.

What would you say to Jesus if he came to your house?

Do you know someone who is ill? Ask Jesus to help them.

5 Put the story in order, punch holes down the left-hand side and tie loosely. Tie 'Jesus' on a length of knitting wool to one of the holes.

6 Move the Jesus figure to every page as you tell the story.

---

1 Make up a scroll to use as an example: tape a few sheets of paper together along the short sides. Tape a piece of dowelling to both ends of the long strip. Write 'God's book' along the paper. Roll up the scroll from both ends with the writing inside.

2 Say that King Josiah was sad that God's Temple building was messy and broken down. He set men to work to make it beautiful again. One of the workers found an old book. (*Show the scroll and unroll it.*) Say: 'Look! It is God's book.'

3 Say that the book was read out to King Josiah. Josiah heard what God had to say and he was sad. He and the people had not been doing what God wanted. Josiah read the book out to the people. They all promised God that they would try to do what God wanted.

4 Allocate parts of the story for the children to draw on individual pages: a worker finding the book; the servant bringing the book to Josiah; Josiah looking sad; Josiah reading the book to the people; the people making the promise to God.

5 Gather the pictures together. Put them in order and tape together. Tape pieces of dowelling on either end as before. Unroll it and tell the story again, encouraging the children to talk about their pictures.

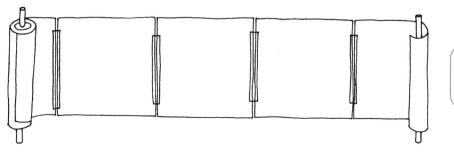

What do we call God's book?

What is your favourite story from God's book?

Bubble blowing

Bubbles can enchant and delight everyone, from the youngest baby to the oldest great-grandparent! There is something wonderful and inspiring about producing a perfect sphere that shines and glistens. You can watch them float and glide, try to catch them on your sleeve or jump up and down to catch and pop them. You can blow small bubbles or large ones, single bubbles or whole strings. Teach young children how to blow gently but firmly and keep persevering. Alternatively, you could just wave the bubble wand and let the air do the work!

Make your own bubble mixture

You will need:
concentrated washing-up or baby-bath liquid, glycerine, warm water, a bucket or bowl, bubble wands (anything circular to make bubbles with), clean water (to rinse the bubble wands and clean down the area, if outside), paper towel

This recipe makes a generous quantity of bubble mixture, ideal for groups of children to play with outdoors.

Put warm water into a bowl or bucket. Gently stir in about a quarter of a bottle of concentrated washing-up liquid and add a good dash of glycerine. Try not to froth it up. There are many variables when making bubble mixture so it's best to experiment to see if the mixture is working. You may need to add more washing-up liquid.

Glycerine from a pharmacy is cheaper than buying tiny bottles used for cake icing. It is not essential but it gives more shimmer and better surface tension to the bubbles.

You can buy all shapes and sizes of bubble wands and gadgets but here are some cheaper alternatives:

● Show children how to make a circle by touching the tip of one index finger to the tip of their thumb. Get everyone to dip their hand in bubble mixture and bring it out slowly. See the film of mixture across the circle. Blow gently at the film and see the bubbles fly.

● Use the plastic circles from multi-packs of cans to blow large and small bubbles at the same time.

● Dip one end of a drinking straw in the mixture and blow from the other end to make tiny bubbles.

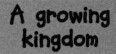

A growing kingdom

Large and small bubbles
Matthew 13:31,32

no limit

You will need:
bubble solution, bubble wands, materials for making a giant bubble wand, such as chenille wires or florists' wire

Jesus goes to heaven

Floating bubbles
Acts 1:9–11

no limit

You will need:
bubble solution, bubble wands

God knows me

Words and actions
Psalm 139

10 mins

You will need:
bubble solution, bubble wands

1 Blow a string of bubbles. Say: 'Look! Lots and lots of bubbles!' Let the children have a go. Say: 'There are lots of people in God's family, too. Some are big and some are small.' Every time the children blow lots of bubbles, comment on how there are 'lots of people in God's family.'

2 Now try to blow a giant bubble. If you do not have a giant bubble wand, make one by twisting a chenille wire or florist's wire into a large circle and twist on another one to make a handle. Ask the children to watch the bubble growing bigger and bigger. Let it float away before it bursts. (This may take a bit of practice!)

3 Let the children have a go at blowing a giant bubble. As the bubbles get bigger, say, 'This is just how God's family is growing. It's always getting bigger and bigger. More and more people are becoming friends with God every day.'

4 Let the children carry on trying to blow strings of bubbles and giant bubbles. Keep reminding them that there are lots of people in God's family and it is always getting bigger.

> Can you blow lots of small bubbles and big bubbles?
>
> Who do you know in God's family?

---

1 Explain that, after Jesus had died, he came alive again. His friends saw him move, heard him speak, felt his body and watched him eat. He was definitely alive. But, after a while, it was time for Jesus to go back to his father, God, in heaven.

2 Go outside and blow some bubbles. Watch them floating up into the sky. Comment on how beautiful the bubbles look, shining and reflecting the light. Watch as the bubbles disappear from sight.

3 Encourage the children to blow bubbles. Ask them to think about Jesus going up to heaven.

(TIP) *Try to choose a day when there is a gentle breeze for this activity. If the bubbles pop, comment on how Jesus suddenly vanished from sight!*

> How do you think Jesus' friends felt when he said he was leaving?
>
> How do you think they felt when they watched him go to heaven?

---

1 Tell the children to sit down and listen to a special song from the Bible. Ask another leader to read the words aloud, while you do the actions with the bubbles:

You know me, God.

You know when I am lying down. *(Lie down and blow bubbles.)*

You know when I am sitting, *(Sit up and blow bubbles.)*

and when I get up. *(Get up and blow bubbles.)*

If I go up to the heavens, you are there. *(Blow bubbles upwards.)*

If I go down to the depths, you are there. *(Blow bubbles downwards.)*

Wherever I go, you are there. *(Blow bubbles while you spin round.)*

You made me inside my mother. *(Gradually, blow a big bubble and let it float away.)*

You made me in a wonderful way. *(Repeat.)*

You are amazing, God! Your thoughts are like thousands of bubbles! *(Blow strings of bubbles.)*

When I do bad things, forgive me. *(Blow a bubble and pop it.)*

Help me to follow you. *(Blow a bubble upwards and another to follow it.)*

2 You could repeat this and get the children to copy the bubble-blowing actions. It may take some practice but you can all have fun trying!

> What do you want to say to God?
>
> How does it feel to think that God knows all about you?

Cards

At special times of the year, cards are an easy craft to make and use as a gift – the most obvious occasions being Christmas, Easter, Mothering Sunday and birthdays. However, there are other times when handmade cards from the group are appreciated, such as 'Get well' cards for people who are ill; or a 'Welcome to the family' card to give to a child at a dedication or baptism service. Cards are fun to make, they allow us to enjoy colours and textures and express our God-given creativity, and they will be treasured by those who receive them.

- Make sure you have one adult to supervise a maximum of six children: more help is required if using glitter or small items (see page 7).

- Use A4 card, folded over. (The smaller the card, the more difficult it is for a young child to work with.) Vary the design by having the fold at the side, the top, or folding both sides into the middle like doors.

- As making cards and scrapbooks are popular hobbies, you will find a wide selection of accessories available in craft shops, stationers and departmental stores. Textured, metallic or patterned sheets of paper and card, stamps and stickers can all be used imaginatively (and in small quantities) to create beautiful cards at little expense. But, tissue paper, glitter, metallic confetti, oddments of gift wrap, coloured cellophane and glitter glue pens are also useful – and can often be found cheaply!

- Create three-dimensional effects by mounting a child's work onto background sheets of metallic or special effect paper with craft foam pads. Use scissors with patterned blades to trim the edges of the paper.

- Save time by printing the wording for the cards onto large labels before the session. Stick one inside each card for the child to complete with their name.

- Card-making enables children to show their love, thanks or concern for someone else. They enjoy being creative and, when they give the card away, they realise they have made someone else happy too.

Naomi and Ruth

Diamond and heart card
Ruth 1

10–15 mins

You will need:
sheets of A4 card, card diamond shapes, heart-shaped stickers, large squares of metallic or corrugated card, small squares of textured or printed paper, white glue, double-sided tape, craft foam pads, glitter or metal confetti, pre-prepared sticky labels (or slips of paper) with appropriate wording

The Christmas baby

A Christmas present
Luke 1:26–38;
Matthew 1:18–23

15 mins

You will need:
A4 green, red or yellow card (folded with the fold at the top), gift tags with the words 'With love, from God' written on, a small rosette (optional), strips of coloured paper or ribbon, self-adhesive stars or a small Christmas design stamp block and metallic stamp pad, large star shapes, pictures of nativity scenes (a stable, baby in a manger), white glue

Jesus is alive

Happy Easter cards
Luke 24:1–12

15 mins

You will need:
A4 pastel-coloured card folded, flowers and leaves, (foam, self-adhesive, silk or dried), crayons or felt-tip pens, butterfly stickers (optional), white glue, circles of card 4 cm in diameter in shades of skin colour, patterned scissors, labels or slips of paper with these phrases on: 'Smile!', 'Happy Easter' and 'Jesus is alive', paper springs (two strips of paper folded together concertina style)

1 Give everyone a diamond shape. Encourage them to decorate it with a heart sticker, put glue around it and sprinkle with glitter or metal confetti.

2 While the shapes are drying, get each child to choose a folded card, one card square and one paper square.

3 Help everyone to attach the card square to the folded card (use double-sided tape if

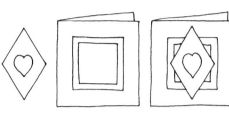

using textured card) and then glue the paper square on top of it. Chat about how much Ruth loved Naomi and wanted to make her happy. Explain that, by making beautiful cards, the children are showing their love for the people who will receive them. Encourage the children to tell you about the people they love.

4 Help the children to fix the diamond on top of the squares, with craft foam pads to give a three-dimensional effect.

5 Hand out labels or paper with appropriate wording to stick inside the card. Remember to allow plenty of space to write names. Encourage the children to write their name inside the cards.

6 Admire all the cards. Tell the children how much their hard work and love will be appreciated by those who receive them, just as Naomi was pleased by everything Ruth did to help her.

 Adapt this design for different occasions using a star, heart or flower shape.

Draw lots of kisses on the card to say: 'I love you!'

---

1 Give out sheets of card folded in half with the fold at the top. Get everyone either to print a motif all over the card or to stick on self-adhesive stars to create a wrapping paper design. Discuss how exciting it is at Christmas to give and receive presents.

2 Help the children to glue two contrasting strips crossways onto the card to represent a ribbon on a parcel. Add a rosette and a gift tag.

3 Explain that, at the first Christmas, God gave a very special present to the world. What was it? The message the angel gave Mary and Joseph was that

Mary was going to have a baby – and her baby would be God's Son!

4 Suggest the children write lots of kisses on the tag to show that God gave his special present because he loved everybody so much.

5 Inside the card, help the children to stick a large star centrally at the top and draw or stick a nativity scene underneath it.

6 Hand out labels or slips of paper with a Christmassy message on. Help everyone to stick them in and write their name.

 Use Christmas-design sticky tape instead of card strips and cut out pictures and 'Happy Christmas' wording from used greetings cards.

What was the baby's name?

What would you like to say to God for giving us such a wonderful present?

---

1 Before the activity:

• Print or write the words on white paper and cut round them with patterned scissors. (Four-year-olds might like to cut out their own greeting.)

• Cut circles of card, 4 cm in diameter for the faces. Remember to include different skin colour.

• Fold some paper springs in a zigzag style.

2 Encourage the children to decorate the front of the card with flowers, leaves and

Jesus' friends had a wonderful surprise on the first Easter Day. Make this card to tell someone what it was.

butterflies. Talk about Mary and her friends going to the garden where Jesus was buried. Were they feeling happy or sad?

3 Give each child a circle of card. Ask them to draw a smiley face on it.

4 Fasten one end of the paper spring securely with tape or glue to the inside of the card (as shown) and attach the smiley face to the other end. Above the face, help the children to glue the word: 'Smile!' Then below it, the phrase: 'Jesus is alive'.

5 Show how, when the card is opened, the smiley face will pop out and make someone feel surprised and happy, just like Jesus' friends felt when the angel told them that Jesus was alive.

6 Encourage everyone to glue the words 'Happy Easter' on the front or inside. Help

the child to complete the card by writing their name.

 Print multiple copies of words on a computer printer, to save time. Only use capital letters at the start of sentences and names.

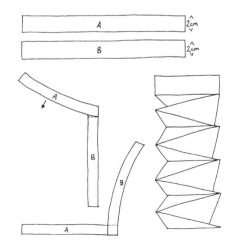

Chalk

Chalks can be used both indoors and outdoors. For activities outdoors, use big chunky chalks, which are easy for small hands to manage. Try chalking on walls, bricks, stones, paving stones, concrete and tarmac. The chalk can be washed off with a hosepipe or wait for it to rain. Alternatively, give the children large paintbrushes and let them 'paint' over the chalk with water. The colours turn much brighter when mixed with water and will run down vertical surfaces which will be fascinating to the children.

Indoors, chalk can be used on chalkboards or coloured paper. You can create a chalkboard by painting a large, flat piece of wood with specialist paint. Try rubbing the chalk with your finger to make a blurred edge or try using the side of the chalk to create a block of colour. Chalks are a messy medium to use, so make sure you cover the children with aprons and provide hand-washing facilities afterwards.

Children enjoy using chalk because it is easy to make a mark, and they can work on a large scale. It is easy to rub something out and start again, whether inside with a board rubber or cloth, or outside with water. Remind the children that this is not the case with pens, crayons, felt-tip pens and paints!

Light of the world

Abstract drawing
Matthew 5:14–16

5 mins

You will need:
a sheet of black paper or chalkboard for each child, white chalk

Being forgiven

Making a clean start
Psalm 51

10 mins

You will need:
chalk, a chalkboard or hard surface outdoors, damp cloth or buckets of water and sponges

Crossing the River Jordan

Drawing the story
Joshua 3

10 mins

You will need:
coloured chalk, a chalkboard, a board rubber
or cloth

1 Give each child a chalkboard or sheet of black paper and a piece of white chalk.

2 Show the children how to draw a circle in the centre of the board or paper and colour it in densely. How does it look against the dark background? Does it stand out? It looks a bit like a light.

3 Show the children how to use their fingers to smudge the chalk and make it radiate out to the edges of the paper. Does this look like the light spreading out? Can you make the light reach to the corners of the paper? You may need to add more chalk to the circle of light first.

4 Say that Jesus wants us to be a bit like that. He wants us to be like lights, shining and reaching out to other people.

5 Cover the chalk lights with black paper. What happens when the light is covered up? Can you see it?

Is the light doing any good? No. Jesus wants us to be lights that can be seen. He wants people to see the good things we do and know that we do them because we are friends with Jesus.

How many different lights can you think of?

See what difference a night light or torch can make in a dark room.

---

1 This activity would be fun to do outside in a large space. However, you could also do it on a board indoors.

2 Say that sometimes we all do things we shouldn't do. (You could give an example such as getting cross or being selfish. Try to choose something that children can relate to, but keep it short and simple.) Then you feel sad and sorry. Draw a large, sad face with the chalk.

3 Ask the children if they ever do things they shouldn't do? How do they feel about it? Can they draw sad and sorry faces too?

4 Say that God forgives us when we are sorry. He washes away the bad things and cleans us on the inside. If you are doing the activity outdoors, give the children buckets of water and sponges to clean off the sad faces. If you are inside, use damp cloths to wipe the sad faces away.

5 Say: 'God gives us a new start. He forgives us and loves us.' Encourage the children to draw happy, smiley faces.

You could talk to Jesus, too and tell him you are sorry.

Everyone gets things wrong sometimes – even grown-ups!

---

1 Tell the children that you are going to tell them a story using the chalkboard and chalk. Afterwards, they can try to retell the story.

2 Draw lots of stick people at the top of the board. Say: 'These are God's people.

God has promised to give them a special land to live in. But there is one problem. A big river is in the way.'

3 Draw lots of wavy blue lines across the board to represent the river. Ask: 'How could the people get across?' Say: 'God had a plan. He told some of the people to carry his special holy box into the river.'

4 Draw a box with twelve people in the middle of the river. Say: 'The water was very deep. What would happen next?'

5 Use the rubber or cloth to rub away some of the blue river to create a path where the people with the box are standing. Say: 'God made a dry path through the middle of the river so all the people could walk across.' Rub out the people at the top of the board and redraw them at the bottom of the board, to show that they have crossed the river.

What do you want to say to this amazing God?

Can you think of any other stories in the Bible with water?

15

Clay

Working with clay is messy and needs thorough cleaning up, but it is fantastic fun and well worth the effort. Using clay helps children to develop coordination and stimulates their imagination and creativity. Be generous with quantities, so that the children can have enough to really get to grips with. They will love the feel and texture, and will be happy shaping and moulding without necessarily making anything recognisable! Using clay will give good opportunity to chat and build relationships as you sit at the table. Talk about how God has given us hands to touch and feel and work with, as well as about the Bible story or topic.

Use 'air hardening clay' which does not need firing. It can be bought at educational suppliers, and art and craft shops.

- Cover all working surfaces with cheap heavy-duty plastic sheeting. Dispose of this afterwards rather than trying to clean it. Keep clay away from soft furnishings and carpets. Lay a 'path' of plastic sheeting from the work area to the clean-up area so clay is not trodden everywhere.

- Cover up the children too! Plastic aprons are ideal.

- Put out some bowls of water for the children to wet their hands before working with the clay. This will make it much easier for them.

- Make a 'slicer' from a piece of string or wire tied to two cotton reels to cut off individual pieces of clay for children to work with.

- Provide bowls of warm clean water for rinsing hands; do not use soap until most of the clay has been eased off; dry hands thoroughly. Use baby lotion afterwards to keep young skin soft. (Check for allergies first.)

- Filter washing water through a sieve before pouring it away; use plenty more water to swill down. (You will not be popular if your cleaning blocks the drains!)

- Store clay to be used in the future in an airtight container, wrapped in polythene to prevent it drying out. Mix in a little water from time to time if the clay is being kept for several weeks.

- Leave clay objects to dry thoroughly; they can then be painted or varnished. Poster paint is suitable – watery paints tend to soften the surface and spoil the finish.

Jeremiah and the potter

Thumb pots
Jeremiah 18:1–12

15–20 mins

You will need:
air-hardening clay, cover-up and clean-up equipment

The Lord's Prayer

Praying as Jesus said
Luke 11:2–4

15–20 mins

You will need:
air-hardening clay, small paper plates, cover-up and clean-up equipment

Ten rules from God

Patterns with purpose
Exodus 19:16 – 20:17

15 mins

You will need:
air-hardening clay, rolling pins, flat craft sticks, cover-up and clean-up equipment

1 Prepare the room and the children for using clay.

2 Tell the children they are going to help you to tell a story about one of God's friends, Jeremiah. Say that one day Jeremiah went to the potter's house to watch him make pots with clay.

3 Give each child some clay. Tell them they are going to be the potter and should act the part as you say the following: 'The potter began to make a pot and Jeremiah watched him. After a while the potter realised the pot was not right, so he squashed up the clay and started again. God told Jeremiah, "The potter is in charge of that clay. He can make what he likes with it. I am in charge of people. I can do what I like." Jeremiah knew that whatever God did would be right, and, if people tried to live his way, he would help them.'

4 Help the children to make simple thumb pots. Make a ball of clay; push thumbs into the middle and gradually build up the sides as the clay is turned around. As the children make their pots, remind them that God works with us, making us into better people and more like him.

> What does clay feel like?
>
> Say thank you to God for helping us to be better people.

---

1 Tell the children that one day Jesus' friends asked him how they should talk to God. Read Luke 11:2–4 and encourage the children to do these actions:

Jesus said that God wants us to praise him. 'Father, may your holy name be honoured; may your kingdom come.' (*Lift hands high.*)

Jesus said God wants us to ask him for our daily food. 'Give us day by day the food we need.' (*Hold out cupped hands.*)

Jesus said God wants us to say sorry when we have done wrong things and to forgive other people. 'Forgive us our sins, (*Put hands by sides and bow heads.*) just as we forgive everyone who does us wrong.' (*Shake or hold hands with someone else.*)

2 Practise the actions, before saying the whole prayer through again.

3 Say to the children that they are going to use their hands again to make something to remember part of Jesus' prayer. Get the children to put aprons on. Encourage each child to use the clay to make food items to put on a paper plate. Remind them not to eat the 'food'!

4 Say the prayer again, this time holding or pointing to the plates of food at the appropriate moment.

> What do you enjoy eating?
>
> Remember to talk to God any time you want!

---

1 Tell the children that Moses was the leader of God's people. He was taking them to their new land. They arrived at a mountain and God said he wanted to speak to the people there. They were to wait at the bottom of the mountain while Moses climbed up to hear what God wanted to say. God gave Moses ten rules to help people to live his way. The rules told the people to praise and trust God, and to be good to each other. The ten rules were carved out on two big blocks of stone for Moses to carry down the mountain.

2 Say that people who love God try to live by his rules today: to praise and trust him, and be good to each other. Tell the children that, to remind them about God's rules, they are going to carve in some clay that looks like stone.

3 Prepare the children and give out the clay. Help them to roll out and shape the

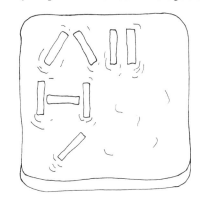

clay. Encourage them to make patterns, pictures or 'writing' using the sticks.

4 Display all the 'stones'. Say a prayer together: 'Thank you, God, for making rules to help us to live your way.'

> What can you do to praise God?
>
> How could you be good to someone you know?

Collage

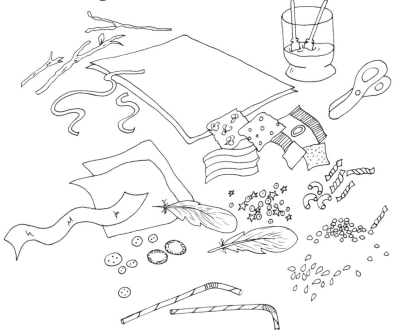

A collage is a picture made out of different materials. The materials can be anything you like, including all types of paper, card, fabric, ribbon, buttons, feathers, sequins, straws, craft sticks, seeds, twigs, lentils, pasta and milk bottle tops. Build up a collection of materials either from specialist craft shops or from bits and pieces around the home. For example, you could save used wrapping paper, sweet wrappers, old magazines and cards. Try to keep your collection in an organised way so that the different materials do not get muddled up. One idea is to use an old biscuit tin for very small items and put different materials in the plastic compartments that once held the different biscuits. Larger items can be stored in different stackable plastic cartons such as the ones used for mushrooms or tomatoes in supermarkets.

Collage is a good way of recycling old and otherwise unwanted materials. You can teach the children the good habit or reusing materials. Show them that what might be viewed as 'rubbish' can be used to make a beautiful picture. This is an illustration of how God can make ordinary things beautiful as well as having a strong environmental message.

Collage can be quite messy so you will need to cover the children and tables, and provide washing facilities. Use a good strong adhesive such as 'white' or 'school' glue and glue spreaders, as some of the materials will be too heavy for a glue stick to work. When you have finished, lift the picture up to check that all the bits are firmly fixed on and then leave it to dry.

Younger children may need the pieces to be pre-cut but let the older children do some cutting for themselves. Individual collages are popular but group ones have the added bonus of working together and producing something much bigger than could be achieved alone.

Moses and the burning bush

Using mixed media
Exodus 3

15* mins

You will need:
a large sheet of card for the background; twigs and leaves; red, yellow and orange tissue paper; paper; crayons; white glue; sticky tape

*add time to collect twigs

Peter meets Jesus

Catching fish
Luke 5:1–11

15 mins

You will need:
a large sheet of blue paper or card, fish shapes cut out from paper, scissors, white glue and spreaders, net or string, collage materials such as silver foil, lentils, sequins

Solomon

Building the Temple
1 Kings 6; 2 Chronicles 3

10 mins

You will need:
a large sheet of card; wooden craft sticks; gold paper; gold paint or fabric; brown paper; sequins; blue, purple or crimson fabric or paper; scissors; white glue and spreaders

1 You could collect the twigs and leaves, with the children, or have them ready. If you do not want to use real twigs and leaves, you could cut them out of paper.

2 Tell the children that you are going to create a picture of a bush. Use the sticky tape to stick the twigs onto the bottom of the card. Try to choose small, straight twigs that will lie fairly flat. Use sticky tape to fasten the leaves in the gaps between the twigs.

3 Say: 'A man called Moses once saw a bush that was a bit like this. But this bush was on fire.' Get the children to tear strips of tissue paper and glue them on, as if radiating out from the bush, to look like flames. Say: 'The bush was on fire, but none of the branches or leaves were getting burned up.'

4 Tell the children that God suddenly spoke to Moses from the burning bush. God had a special job for Moses to do. Ask a child to draw a picture of Moses to put next to the bush.

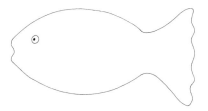
Can you find out what special job God had for Moses?

Moses talked to God in the burning bush but we can talk to God anywhere.

1 Give each child a fish shape. Make them as large as possible but small enough to fit them all onto your background sheet.

2 Provide the children with collage scraps and encourage them to decorate their fish as simply or elaborately as they like.

3 Ask the children to glue their finished fish onto the large sheet of paper. Comment on what a lot of fish there are.

4 Say: 'Jesus helped a man called Peter, who was a fisherman. Peter hadn't caught any fish for hours and hours. But Jesus told him to throw his net on the other side of the boat.' Glue the net over the fish or stick on criss-crossing lengths of string to make a net.

5 Say: 'Peter caught so many fish that day, his net nearly broke! He was amazed and became a friend of Jesus that very day.'

Why do you think Peter threw his net on the other side, like Jesus said?

How many fish were in the net you made?

---

1 Say: 'There was once a good king called Solomon. He wanted to build a very special Temple for God. We are going to make a picture of this beautiful building.' Let the children help to build up the collage.

2 Say: 'Solomon planned for the floor of the Temple to be made out of wood' (1 Kings 6:15a). Help the children to glue the craft sticks at the bottom of the picture.

3 Say: 'Solomon covered the inside of the Temple …with gold' (1 Kings 6:22). Get the children to cover the rest of the background with gold paper.

4 Say: 'Solomon's helpers carved two great big creatures with wide wings, from wood. They covered them in gold' (1 Kings 6:23–28). Cut out two shapes, a bit like lions with their wings spread out, from the brown paper. Get the children to paint or cover them with gold. Ask a child to stick these in the middle of the picture.

5 Say: 'Next to these, was a curtain made of blue, purple and crimson fabric' (2 Chronicles 3:14). Allow another child to glue this on.

6 Say: 'Solomon covered the whole place with precious stones' (2 Chronicles 3:6). Invite everyone to glue the sequins all over the gold. What a beautiful building Solomon made for God!

Have you ever seen a building like the Temple?

What do you think God thought of this building made for him?

Cooking (with heat)

Cooking is a worthwhile, sociable and fun activity. It involves children working together in cooperation, to make food to share with one another. Cooking extends children's sensory awareness through their touching, smelling and tasting of the food.

Handling a variety of ingredients and watching them being transformed into something else, communicates something of the wonder of God's world. And, just as in Bible times, the creation of food, even a complete meal, and sharing it together, can be an important part of a special festival or celebration.

Keep the safety of the children in mind at all times. Careful assessment of risks and thorough planning will make this a safe, and enjoyable activity.

See page 22 for advice on hygiene, equipment safety, allergies and food safety.

- Encourage the children to be as 'hands-on' as possible. Don't let them handle food in and out of the oven, of course (see 'Equipment safety' page 22), but do involve them in as many processes as you can.

- Work in small groups so that each child is guaranteed a turn: four, with a leader, is ideal. If your group is larger, split into smaller groups and have an adult with each or repeat the activity with a different small group each time.

- Involve the children in the cleaning-up process too. To a child, this is at least as much fun as the cooking!

- Be prepared. Have everything ready. Choose simple recipes that require a minimum of ingredients and equipment, and that give good results, with limited adult input. Keep healthy eating in mind.

- Have a leader who takes responsibility for using the oven and handling hot items. Let children watch, from a distance. Make sure there is a leader present who has a First Aid qualification.

- Think carefully about the timing. Choose recipes that you can complete (and eat, if you wish) within the time span of the group session. Remember, it will take longer than when you make it yourself!

- Share the children's pleasure at the results of their labours!

Moses is safe

Making baskets and babies
Exodus 2:1–10

 15* mins

You will need:
a saucepan, a wooden spoon, a 15 ml measuring spoon, a large bowl

Ingredients:	
60 g margarine	Shredded bran or wheat breakfast cereal (about 12 heaped spoonfuls)
2 spoons of golden syrup	
4 heaped spoons of drinking chocolate powder	Marzipan (but be aware of nut allery sufferers) or fondant icing

*add time for cooling

Jesus is baptised

'Coventry God-cakes'
Mark 1:9–13

30* mins

You will need:
a rolling pin, a round-ended knife, a spoon, a pastry brush

Ingredients:	
ready-made puff pastry	mincemeat
	a small amount of flour
	a small cup of milk

*15 minutes prep, 15 minutes cooking

Jesus feeds a crowd

Gingerbread people
Luke 9:10–17

 30* mins

You will need:
a large and a small bowl, a sieve, a wooden spoon, a metal spoon, a rolling pin, shaped cutters, a flat knife, baking sheets, a cooling rack

Ingredients:	
500 g plain flour	4 large spoonfuls of golden syrup
10 g ground ginger	10 g baking powder
200 g soft brown sugar	150 g margarine
	1 egg

*15 minutes prep, 15 minutes cooking

1 Put the margarine and golden syrup into a saucepan. Melt over a low heat.

2 Add the drinking chocolate. Stir well. Take the saucepan away from the heat.

3 Put the cereal in a bowl. Pour on the chocolate mixture and stir well to cover all the cereal.

4 Let the mixture cool. Give each child a few spoonfuls. Let them press this together to form a basket shape. Encourage everyone to pretend to be Moses' mother as they make the baskets. Praise the children for taking care, just as Moses' mother took care when she was making the basket to carry her baby. Leave the baskets in a cool place to set.

5 Give each child a piece of marzipan or fondant icing to shape into a baby. Encourage everyone to wrap the baby in another flat piece of marzipan or icing and put him in their basket. Chat about the Bible story. Why did Moses' mother make the basket? Do the children think baby Moses will be safe?

 Quick method: Replace stages 1 and 2 by melting chocolate in a bowl, over a bowl of hot water.

> Who looked after baby Moses and kept him safe?
>
> What do you want to say to God?

These cakes were traditionally given to children by their godparents when they were confirmed.

1 Sprinkle a little flour onto a work surface. Get the children to help you roll out the puff pastry, quite thinly.

2 Cut squares of pastry, roughly 15 cm x 15 cm, and give one to each child. Ask them to count how many corners there are to the square.

3 Put a spoonful of mincemeat in the centre of each square. Get the children to fold the pastry diagonally to form a triangle, pressing the edges down with a little milk to make them stick.

4 Make three small cuts in the top of each parcel. Help the children to brush a little milk over the surface. Challenge the children to count how many corners and slits there are now. (Three!) Put the cakes into a hot oven for about 15 minutes or until the pastry has risen and browned.

5 While the cakes are cooking and cooling, tell the Bible story of Jesus' baptism. Follow the tradition of giving the children a cake and say that the three corners represent Jesus who was baptised, the Holy Spirit who appeared as a dove, and God who said he was pleased with Jesus.

 This activity will not teach children the complex doctrine of the Trinity but they will start to become familiar with these words and names which they may not otherwise encounter.

> Think about God. Isn't he amazing?!

---

1 Briefly tell, in your own words, the story of Jesus feeding 5,000 people. Suggest that you could make a crowd of people together. Make sure that your hands, working surfaces and equipment are clean before you start.

> How many 'people' have you made in your crowd of gingerbread people?
>
> Can you remember how many people Jesus fed?

2 Sieve the flour, baking powder and ginger into a large bowl. Get the children to rub in the margarine with their fingers. Stir in the sugar.

3 Break the egg into a small bowl. Add the syrup and stir well together. (Using a slightly warmed metal spoon will make this easier.)

4 Add the egg mixture to the large bowl. Invite a child to help you mix it together well. Everyone can help to squeeze it into a dough.

5 Tip the dough out onto a clean floured working surface. Give a piece to each child to roll out and cut into shape. These quantities will make 15–20 gingerbread people, but remember that smaller

children will need larger quantities to work with.

6 Place the 'people' on a greased baking sheet and bake for 10–15 minutes or until golden brown. Thicker shapes will take longer to cook. Loosen from the sheets while still warm and leave to cool.

7 When the 'people' are cool enough to handle, hold them up while you tell the story again.

Cooking (no heat)

Children love cooking, but time and facilities do not always allow for food preparation, cooking, cooling and eating. This section gives you some recipes to try that do not need heat.

Hygiene:

- Always wash your hands before handling food.
- Clean all surfaces with an anti-bacterial cleaner.
- Make sure that all utensils are clean.
- When possible, let the children make their own individual items.

Equipment safety:

- Take care using knives; table knives are safest.
- Keep flexes, kettles and pan handles out of the reach of children.
- Try to do as much as possible at the children's height; do not encourage children to stand on chairs to reach the working area.
- Put a damp cloth or rubber mat under a mixing bowl to prevent it slipping.
- Choose sturdy equipment and teach the children to use it safely.

Allergies and food safety:

- Be aware of the food sensitivities of your group. Check with their parents or carers beforehand for allergies to ingredients, additives or flavourings.
- Be cautious when using recipes including nuts, as some children have serious reactions to them.
- Small children can choke very easily so take care when sharing food together.
- Avoid recipes involving raw eggs.
- Ensure all ingredients are fresh and have been properly stored. Your local environmental health services will be pleased to advise you.

See page 20 for general advice on cooking.

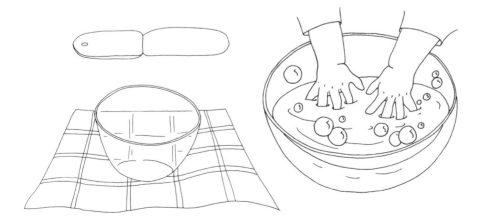

Iced biscuits
Luke 10:38–42

5–10 mins

You will need:
paper or plastic plates, bowls, teaspoons, a large spoon, biscuits, icing sugar, water, cake decorations or sweets

God made fruit

Fruit salad
Genesis 1:11–13

10 mins

You will need:
chopping board(s), a large bowl, small bowls, table knives, a sharp knife, spoons, a variety of fruit

God gives food

Manna
Exodus 16:31

5–10 mins

You will need:
paper plates, a bowl, food wrap, a damp cloth or wet wipes for sticky fingers, flaked breakfast cereal, honey (runny), icing sugar in sugar shakers, honey drizzler or metal spoon

1 In a bowl, mix the icing sugar with water, a little at a time. Let the children stir it with a large spoon. Make sure each child has a turn. Add more icing sugar or water to create a stiff mixture.

2 Give each child a biscuit on a plate. Put the cake decorations in different bowls.

3 Let the children use the teaspoons to spread the icing mixture on the biscuits; then add the cake decorations. The biscuits look like a special treat for someone. Ask: 'Do your mums and dads make special food for special visitors?'

4 Say that Martha had a very special visitor coming – Jesus. She wanted the house and the food to be just right for

him. Perhaps she made some special biscuits like these. Explain that, when Jesus arrived, she still carried on getting ready. Martha's sister, Mary, stopped her work to listen to Jesus, and that made Martha cross. She was left to do all the work!

Who was right – Martha or Mary? Why?

Ask someone to read you this story about Jesus while you eat your special biscuit.

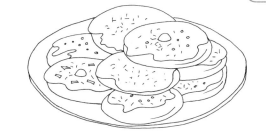

---

1 Try to provide as large a variety of fruit as possible. Think about including seasonal and more unusual fruits.

2 Show the children the fruit and pass it round for them to touch and smell. Do the children know what the fruits are? Have they ever tried them? Talk about all the different colours, shapes and textures.

3 Demonstrate cutting up and peeling the fruit. Allow the children to do as much as possible, using blunt knives.

4 Talk about the seeds inside the fruit, from tiny grape seeds to large peach stones. What

do the seeds do? What would happen if you planted them?

5 Put chunks of fruit into a big bowl and let the children mix them up with a spoon to make a fruit salad.

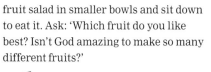

6 Let the children serve themselves some fruit salad in smaller bowls and sit down to eat it. Ask: 'Which fruit do you like best? Isn't God amazing to make so many different fruits?'

 This can get messy, so provide cloths or wet wipes to clean sticky fingers.

Which fruit do you like best?

What do you want to say to God?

---

1 As you lay out the ingredients, chat about the manna that the Israelites tasted in the Bible story: 'God's people "called the bread manna. It was white … and delicious as wafers made with honey" (Exodus 16:31). Nobody really knows what it looked like, but it may have tasted a bit like this…'

Why did God give the Israelites manna?

What food does God give you to eat?

2 Give each child a strong paper plate with their name written clearly on the rim. Pour the cereal into a bowl. Let the children take a handful and put it on their plates.

3 Then bring out the runny honey and icing sugar. Using a honey drizzler, show the children how to cover their flakes with honey. Let each child drizzle on the honey; be on hand to help.

4 Next, let them shake on the icing sugar from a sugar shaker. If possible, have three or four shakers, so that they do not spend long waiting.

5 Once everyone has finished decorating and experimenting, taste the manna. Is it

'delicious', like the real manna in the Bible story?

6 Wrap the individual plates well and keep them ready to hand out at home time.

Cutting and sticking

Children can have more freedom in cutting and sticking and doing 'unstructured' collage work. The emphasis is less on the finished product and more on the process. You can afford to be less fussy about outcome and more concerned with the individual child's effort and progress. Let them have fun and experiment, even if the results do not turn out quite how you expected.

Young children are learning essential fine motor skills, which include learning to use a pair of scissors. Teach them how to insert their thumb and finger(s) into the loops of the scissors. They need to hold the scissors vertically and the paper horizontally. Show them how to open and shut the scissors (practise this pincer movement without the scissors). Children will begin by doing small snips into a sheet of paper. They will progress on to doing more than one snip, to cut in a straight line. Finally, they will learn how to follow a line when cutting, moving the paper rather than the scissors. You will probably have children at all stages in your group.

You need to teach children how to use scissors safely. Emphasise the importance of keeping scissors away from faces and to close them before passing them to someone else. Remind the children that scissors are for paper and card, not clothes and hair! Use round-ended scissors but make sure they are sharp enough to cut properly. Provide a few pairs of left-handed scissors. This may be some children's first experience of using scissors, so make sure it is a positive one!

The activities suggested here have some sort of starting point, depending on what materials you supply and which Bible story you are exploring, but the children can enjoy cutting and sticking freely, within these informal guidelines.

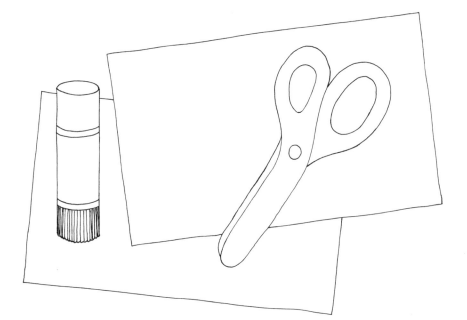

God loves everyone

Peter's dream
Acts 10

10 mins

You will need:
magazines and catalogues with pictures of people, a large sheet of paper, glue, scissors

Abraham's journey

Pack a suitcase
Genesis 12:1–9

15 mins

You will need:
paper, shopping catalogues, food and outdoor-pursuits magazines, glue, sticky tape, scissors

God's rainbow promise

Paper and fabric
Genesis 9:8–17

10–15 mins

You will need:
a large sheet of card or paper, magazines, glue, scissors, coloured paper and fabric scraps in shades of red, orange, yellow, green, blue, indigo/dark blue, purple

1 Give the children the magazines and catalogues. It might be easier to tear out some pages in advance and give each child a page. Provide magazines which show a wide range of ages, genders, cultures and abilities.

2 Encourage the children to cut out lots of different people. Help them, not by doing it for them, but by showing them how to move on to the next stage of cutting.

Who does God love?

Who should we love?

3 Get everyone to glue the pictures onto the large sheet of paper. Say that this reminds you of a dream that a man called Peter once had. In the dream, God told Peter that he loved everyone. It did not matter how old they were or what colour their skin was or what country they came from or whether they were rich or poor.

4 Invite the children to draw a picture of themselves and add it to the picture. Title the picture: 'God loves everyone.'

---

1 This activity will give children the chance to make an individual picture. For each child, prepare a sheet of A4 paper by folding it in half and cutting round the two corners opposite the fold. Open them out. Cut two strips of paper for each child (or ask them to do this if they are capable).

2 Give each child a sheet of A4 paper and two strips. Get everyone to stick the strips on the short sides of the paper as handles. It should look like an open suitcase.

Where would you like to go on a journey?

Wherever you go, God is always with you.

3 Talk to the children about what they would like to pack if they were going on a long journey. Encourage them to find pictures of these in the magazines, cut them out and stick them in their suitcases.

4 Say that a man called Abraham had to go on a long journey. God told him to pack his bags, leave his home and travel to a new country. Abraham did not know where it was, but he knew that God was with him and that everything would be all right. What would Abraham need to take with him? Compare this with what the children have packed in their suitcases.

5 You could set off on an imaginary journey around the room, taking your cases with you. Do they feel very heavy? Have you got everything you need? Are you going to go to a new country, like Abraham did?

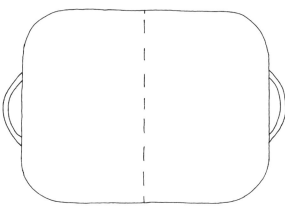

---

1 Cut out a simple outline of a rainbow from the card. (Join several sections together or a strip of lining paper to make a huge rainbow!) Mark on six or seven broad stripes. Seven is more scientifically accurate but can look duller, with large areas of darker colours. Tell the children that God made a promise to a man called Noah. God said he would not send a big flood of water again and he showed Noah a lovely rainbow in the sky as a sign that he had made this promise.

2 Provide the children with lots of coloured paper and fabric. Encourage them to cut off small pieces and glue them onto the rainbow outline, working in huge stripes. This will make a beautiful colourful rainbow, with red on the outermost arc of the shape.

3 Younger children could tear the paper or you could give them thin strips of paper that they can cut across with one snip. Older children may enjoy finding blocks of colour in magazine pictures to cut out.

4 Say that Noah was very happy to see the rainbow. He knew God would keep his promise.

Have you ever seen a rainbow in the sky?

What makes you think about God?

Dough

A dough table provides endless hours of interest, creativity and pleasure. It is relaxing, non-threatening and yet satisfying and exciting, all at the same time. You can buy commercially produced play dough in many colours but it is easy and cheap to make your own. Children love to have generous quantities of dough to handle. Several simple recipes are included on these pages.

The standard dough used here is known as 'salt' or 'baking' dough. It can be used as a moulding dough; it can be cooked slowly to harden, and does not need heat to make. Therefore, it is ideal for children to make themselves, as well as use.

'SALT' OR 'BAKING' DOUGH

1.5 kg plain flour   1.5 kg salt   75 ml cooking oil   1 litre water

Make large quantities of dough so that children can play with generous amounts. This recipe will give you a large bowlful.

1 Mix the flour, salt and oil in a bowl and add the water gradually to make a smooth paste.

2 Knead well on a floured surface, until you have a smooth springy texture. Let the children play with the dough.

3 Cook on a greased baking tray in a medium oven for 20–60 minutes depending on size of model. Or cook overnight on a low heat.

Storage for any home-made dough

Home-made dough can be used again and again, and will keep for several weeks, if stored in a plastic bag or a container with a well-fitted lid.

● If the dough has dried out, try mixing in a little more water.

● If the dough has a salt crust, try kneading in a little more oil.

● If the container is not well sealed, the dough may absorb water from the atmosphere and can get quite sticky. You may be able to add in more flour and save it, but it often needs to go in the bin when it gets to this stage!

● The cream of tartar in some recipes helps to improve the keeping qualities so if you want to keep the dough for reuse, do make sure you include this. If the dough is only for short-term play, it is not so important.

The woman who was forgiven

Baked salt dough
Luke 7:36–50

15* mins

You will need:
a bowl, a wooden spoon, blunt knives, 'salt' or 'baking' dough, greased baking tray
*add cooking time

God chooses Gideon

Salt dough with cutters
Judges 6:11–16

10 mins

You will need:
salt dough (recipe on left), people cutters, rolling pins, modelling tools, mats or boards, a garlic press (optional), paper plates, pen

---

God made animals

Imaginative dough play
Genesis 1:20–25

10 mins

You will need:
salt dough or play dough (recipes above and 28), boards or mats

1 Say that sometimes you do things you shouldn't. Shape some dough into a face, adding extra pieces of dough to show the eyes and a nose. Say: 'When I'm sorry I look like this', and shape a sad mouth using a length of dough.

2 Ask the children if they have ever felt sorry about something. Can they make a sad face too with some dough?

3 Tell them that a woman once came to Jesus. She was so sorry about all the bad things she had done. She cried so much; she made Jesus' feet wet! Can you add tears to the face you made?

4 What do the children think Jesus did? Jesus forgave her, just like he forgives us when we are sorry. Show the children how you can reshape the face with a happy smiling mouth, and no tears.

5 Cook the faces on a greased baking tray in a medium oven for 20–60 minutes

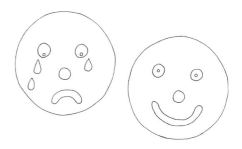

How did the woman in the story show she was sorry?

What do you want to say to God?

(depending on size) until hard, or overnight on a low heat.

6 Let the children take their happy faces home to remind them of Jesus' love and forgiveness.

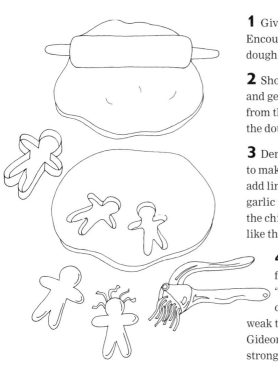

1 Give each child some salt dough. Encourage them to practise rolling the dough with the rolling pins.

2 Show the children the people cutters and get them to cut out people shapes from the dough. Show them how to peel the dough away from the cutters.

3 Demonstrate using the modelling tools to make the eyes, nose and mouth, and add lines for clothing. You could use a garlic press to make strands of hair. Can the children make the dough person look like them?

4 The dough is quite flimsy and fragile, and can break easily. Say: 'The dough people are small. God chose a man, who was small and weak to help him. His name was Gideon. Gideon did not think he was big and strong enough for God to use him. But

God likes to use people who are small and weak – people like Gideon, and like us.'

5 Give each child a paper plate to put their dough person on. Help the children write their names on the plates.

6 Say, 'God chooses …' and ask each child to shout out their name in turn and hold out their plate with the dough person.

What sort of people does God choose?

How does it feel to know that God chooses you?

---

1 Make some salt dough (page 26) or play dough (page 28). The advantage of salt dough is that you can bake it to make a permanent model, although this will take extra time. The advantage of play dough is that you can reuse it another time.

What is your favourite animal?

How do you think God felt about all the animals he made?

2 Give each child some dough on a mat or board. Allow them to play with it freely for a while.

3 Ask the children if they can make some animals, fish or birds with the dough. Allow the children to experiment freely and see what they invent. If they ask for help, you could model rolling out a long thin snake, spiralling a long 'sausage' to make a snail, or pushing eight legs onto a ball of dough to make an octopus.

4 See if the children can invent their own animal. Ask questions like: 'How big is the body?' 'How many legs has it got?'

and 'What is your animal called?' Praise them for their creations.

5 Say that, when God made the world, he made all the different animals. We can make dough animals, but God made real living creatures.

Dough: more recipes and ideas

MOULDING PLAY DOUGH

For each child:

200 g plain flour   100 g salt   10 g cream of tartar   15 ml cooking oil
300 ml water, with added food colouring, if preferred

You will also need a large strong pan and a wooden spoon

1 Put the dry ingredients and oil in the pan.

2 Gradually add the water and colouring, stirring to avoid lumps.

3 Cook over a low heat, stirring all the time, until the mixture thickens and leaves the sides of the pan.

4 Put the dough on a heat-resistant surface and knead. Take care, as it will be hot, especially in the centre of the lump. Soak the pan in cold water.

5 Once the mixture has cooled completely, let the children play with it.

'CERAMIC' PLAY DOUGH

For each child:

two cups of salt   water   one cup of cornflour,

You will also need a measuring cup, a mixing bowl, a large saucepan and a wooden spoon.

1 Gradually mix half a cup of water with one cup of cornflour in the bowl.

2 Mix two-thirds of a cup of water with two cups of salt in the saucepan and cook over medium heat, stirring continuously.

3 Remove the saucepan from the heat after about three minutes, or when bubbles start to form.

4 Immediately, add the water and cornflour mixture, then return to a low heat and stir until smooth.

5 Remove from heat again and allow to cool. Knead the dough until smooth and pliable. It will be whiter than other types of dough. Store in an airtight container, at room temperature.

QUICK DOUGH

For four children:

1.5 kg flour   500 g salt   400 ml water

You will also need a large mixing bowl and a wooden spoon.
This is a recipe the children can make together.

1 Put the ingredients in a bowl and invite the children to mix everything together to make a dough. Add extra flour or water, if necessary.

2 This is not an accurate dough recipe. The type of flour used and even the weather can make the dough vary greatly. Plain flour makes a good basic dough. Self-raising flour is more puffy and springy. Strong flour makes a tough elastic dough; and wholemeal flour gives a gritty grainy dough.

Bread and fish

Moulding play dough
John 6:1–15

You will need:
Moulding play dough (recipe on left)

Presents from the wise men

Glittery, fragrant dough
Matthew 2:1–12

You will need:
Moulding play dough (recipe on left) specially prepared as in step one of the activity; glitter or sequins; vanilla, lemon or peppermint food flavouring; food colouring

God made the sun, moon and stars

'Ceramic' dough
Genesis 1:14–19

You will need:
Ceramic dough (recipe on left), paint or felt-tip pens, glue, glitter, pastry cutters in sun, moon and star shapes (optional), cover-up and clean-up equipment
*add time to harden (about 36 hours)

The parable of the yeast

Quick dough
Matthew 13:33

You will need
Quick dough (recipe on left)
This can be made with the children.
*add time to harden

1 Give the play dough out between the children and invite them to play.

2 As you play, tell the children the story of how Jesus fed 5,000 people with just five loaves and two fishes. Can the children make these with their dough?

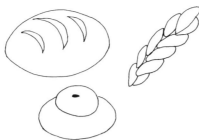

3 Suggest making small round baps, flat pittas and long French sticks. Can the children make a tail and fins for the fish?

4 Select five 'loaves' and two 'fishes' and put them on a plate. Does it look enough to feed five thousand people?

How many people did Jesus feed?

Could anyone else have done this?

---

1 Make the play dough as shown on the left, but add glitter, sequins and food flavouring before heating it. You could make three batches of different colours – one with glitter or sequins and two with different flavourings.

2 Give the children the dough. Can they guess what has been added? They can try

What present would you give to Jesus?

Can you remember the names of the presents the wise men gave?

smelling it (but stress that it is not for eating!).

3 It looks and smells more special than ordinary dough so the children can use it to make some special things. Challenge them to make a ball, a cylinder and a cube from the play dough. Demonstrate, if necessary. If you have made three batches, make a different shape with each batch.

4 Say that these remind you of the presents that the wise men gave to baby Jesus. Do the children know what they were? The gold was a very special,

precious, shiny present like the dough with glitter or sequins. The frankincense and myrrh had lovely fragrances, like the dough with flavourings. They were very special presents for Jesus.

 Do not use perfume or aromatherapy oils – these are too volatile and can damage the skin.

---

1 Give the children the dough to play with freely. After a while, tell the children that when God made the world he made the sun for the daytime and the moon and stars for the night-time. Can the children make these shapes? You could use cutters or mould the dough.

2 Models will take at least 36 hours to harden. They can then be coloured with felt-tip pens or paint. Use glitter and glue to make the stars sparkle.

Larger templates for this activity can be found on pages 81, 82 and 83.

What can you see in the sky?

How many stars do you think God made?

---

1 Once the children have mixed the dough, give them each a piece to knead. Demonstrate how you can squash, press,

When you talk about Jesus, you help God's family to grow.

Try making some real bread and watch the yeast work.

squeeze, pull and knead the dough. Let the children copy you.

2 Say that this is a bit like making bread, but one special ingredient is missing. Do the children know what it is? Yeast is the thing that makes dough grow and become light and fluffy, and ready to be baked as bread. See if the children can stretch the dough as if it is growing.

3 Jesus told a story about a woman who made some bread and made sure the yeast was all mixed in so the bread would grow. God wants us to be like yeast, helping to grow his family.

1 Making a box-television

Follow the instructions to make a simple television out of a cardboard box and enjoy showing your very own television productions.

Make programmes about:
- *your favourite Bible stories*
- *things you want to talk to God about*
- *your home, family and friends*
- *anything at all!*

Or you can photocopy the pictures on the opposite page. Cut them out and stick them onto to a length of paper in story order. Tell the story of Moses and God's people walking through the sea on the dry path that God made for them (Exodus 14:21,22).

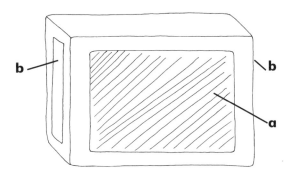

1 Choose a cardboard box, any size. Cut out the shaded area (a) to make the screen. Cut slots at (b) on each side.

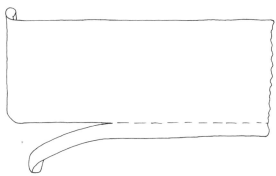

2 Trim a long sheet of paper (old wallpaper is ideal) so that it will go through the slots.

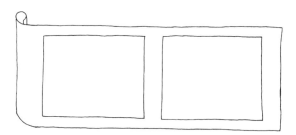

3 Paste pictures along the strip of paper in story order. Leave at least 10 cm blank at each end of the paper and also between each picture.

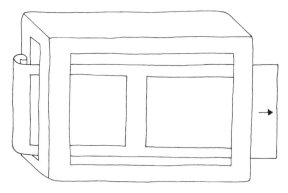

4 Feed the paper through the slots. Enjoy watching your very own television programmes.

Drawing

From earliest history, people have always liked to make their mark. Even young children delight in being able to use a drawing implement.

It is important to have suitable drawing materials for young children to use, like broad wax crayons or chunky felt-tip pens. Avoid pencil crayons, which are too fine a medium for children of this age. Young children need chunky drawing implements that are easy to hold with their little fingers and which quickly put a lot of colour on the page. They also love to explore different drawing tools, like charcoal and oil pastels. Use white on black for something unusual, or try different size and shape papers. Chalk is also popular (either used dry on chalkboards; or soaked overnight in sugar water and used for drawing on paper – see page 14). Drawing in damp sand is also fun.

From 3 years and upwards, encourage the correct pencil grip. It is hard to change later and a poor grip makes handwriting very difficult.

Be aware that young children go through developmental stages of drawing. This is a necessary progression. Even if a child's picture is no more than a scribble, to them it is 'drawing', and we must respect the attempt. To try to correct it, or to draw for them, will damage their confidence. As they continue to have experience with drawing, they will naturally progress, if they have access to drawing materials.

Afterwards, chat to children about their pictures. 'Tell me about your picture,' is always a good and safe starting point. Never tell a child their drawing is 'wrong'. Look for something you can make a positive comment about, such as: 'I see you took the purple crayon and went round and round.' Avoid comments such as: 'I like your picture'. Drawing is self-expression, it's not about pleasing others.

Helping children to learn how to observe objects carefully, naturally develops their drawing. Contemplation is described as taking a 'long loving look at life'. Drawing then is surely a spiritual experience, because it is impossible to draw well without truly looking.

page 14

A man with a damaged hand

Drawing round a hand
Mark 3:1–5

15* mins

You will need:
a sheet of A4 paper per child, felt-tip pens, wax crayons

*less time than this for younger children

Peter and the angel

Mixed media pictures
Acts 12:1–17

15–20 mins

You will need:
a variety of 'angel' pictures, large sheets of good quality paper (one per child); black permanent marker pens; medicine droppers; paint pots; medium brushes; protective aprons; protected working surface; coloured inks: dark blue, red, yellow. (Use a few drops in water. More ink gives a stronger colour. Experiment to get the shades you want. Food colouring is cheaper but it is not as vibrant.)

Palm Sunday

Draw a crowd
Mark 11:1–11

20 mins

You will need:
coloured chalk pre-soaked in sugar water, a long length of lining paper secured to the wall at a suitable height for children to draw on it (or several sheets of flip chart paper taped together), praise music CD and CD-player (optional)

1 Discuss how important our hands are. Look carefully at your own hands. Observe how many fingers and thumbs you have. How are they different? What would happen if we did not have joints on our fingers? (Try picking something up without bending your fingers.) Imagine if we did not have fingers or hands. Look at your fingernails and the position of them: why do we have them? Talk about how wonderfully God has made our hands to help us to do all sorts of things.

2 Tell the story of a man with a damaged hand from Mark 3:1–5.

3 Demonstrate how to spread one hand flat, with fingers apart, on the paper, and draw around the shape. Help the children to do this and to add on details of finger joints, nails, and so on. Could the man in the Bible story draw with his damaged hand? What about when Jesus made his hand better?

 It is great fun to draw around a hand and then to decorate the shape however you like with spots, stripes, flowers, or patterns.

How do you think the man felt when his hand did not work properly?

How did he feel when Jesus made him better?

What do you think was the first thing he did when his hand was better?

---

1 Ask the children what they think angels look like. Tell them a Bible story about an angel from Acts 12:1–17. God sends the angel to look after Peter and rescue him from prison.

2 Look at your pictures of angels. What do the children think of them?

3 Show them an angel you have drawn, with permanent maker. Add stars in the sky to show it is night-time.

4 Paint inside the angel outline using prepared light blue, red and yellow inks. Paint the sky around the angel with dark blue. (Don't worry if the colours run slightly.) Remind the children that God sent the angel to protect Peter. God's angels keep us safe, too.

5 Put your example to one side and encourage the children to devise and draw their own angels.

You can find a larger template of an angel shape on page 80.

 Children must wear protective waterproof aprons to avoid their clothes being stained.

 Think of times when God keeps you safe.

Put your angel picture somewhere to remind you that God's angels are always looking after you.

---

1 Prepare a variety of colours of ordinary chalk, by soaking it overnight in a solution of one part sugar to five parts water. Drain off the water, but use the chalk damp. This gives a very different consistency to dry chalk. (Do a test-run beforehand.) Alternatively, use oil pastels.

2 Share the story of Palm Sunday from Mark 11:1–11. Sing a few celebratory songs, waving imaginary palm leaves, to capture the joyous mood of recognising Jesus as King.

3 Encourage the children to imagine how the street was filled with people, all shouting praises to Jesus. Ask each child to identify a different character who could have been there that they would like to draw. Help the children understand that, no matter how old or young, or whatever we look like, we can all give our praise to Jesus.

4 Give each child a space on the paper and encourage them to draw a large picture of their person. Encourage everyone to stand back to admire the completed scene and sing a song of praise again.

 Play lively contemporary praise music while the children are working, to create and encourage a celebration atmosphere.

Can you make up your own song to sing to Jesus?

Perhaps you can make a dance too?

Glue pictures

Glue pictures are a very useful, versatile art form and can be as easy (or as complicated) as you wish them to be. They are ideal for toddlers as well as preschool children, and always look effective. Adult supervision is required, especially if using glitter. One adult for every four children is best. Use glue pictures as a way of introducing themes, as a reminder of a Bible story, and as a hands-on sensory experience of exploring and enjoying the variety of colours, shapes and textures in God's world.

There are several basic methods:

METHOD A

The simplest method for young children is to make abstract pictures. Put blobs of glue on a sheet of paper and let the children stick collage materials on them. You could include squares and triangles of paper and fabric, pictures cut from used greeting cards, and strands of wool. Try a colour theme, such as shades of purple (Lydia's story); gold, silver and purple (Old Testament kings); or make one picture for each colour of the rainbow (Noah).

METHOD B

1 Draw the outline of a shape on a sheet of thick paper or card. Encourage each child to draw over the shape with glue pens.

2 Get the children to sprinkle fine sand, glitter or sawdust over the paper. Most of this will adhere to the glue, and the remainder can be shaken off and reused.

METHOD C

1 Draw a shape, either freehand or using a template, onto the sheet of paper.

2 Let the children spread glue inside the shape.

3 Provide a selection of materials to stick inside the shape. These could include: tissue paper (circles, squares, strips or scrunched-up bits); sweet wrappers (cellophane or metallic); pasta shapes and pulses; glitter; sawdust; wood shavings; sand.

METHOD D

Provide cut-out shapes (butterflies, fishes, flowers, stars) onto which the child can glue any collage materials. These shapes can be adapted for use as cards or mobiles, if you wish.

 Use a plain paper plate for the background instead of paper.

God's promise to Abraham

A camel from sand
Genesis 22:17

 8 mins

You will need:
A4 sheets of paper, fine sand (preferably in a sieve or flour shaker), white glue or glue pens, a camel template (optional)

Queen Esther

Wear a crown
Esther

15 mins

You will need:
strips of metallic card long enough to wrap round a child's head, jewel-shaped templates, a marker pen, double-sided tape or hair grips, glitter (red, green and blue) or pieces of brightly coloured tissue paper or cellophane

---

Lydia joins the church

Purple abstract collage
Acts 16:11–15

 8–10 mins

You will need:
A4 sheets of paper or card for background (white, lilac, silver), white glue, purple scraps of paper, tissue paper, fabric, cellophane, wool, sweet wrappers and packaging

1 Either freehand or using a template, draw a camel for each child. Some children may be able to draw their own camel, if you help them, by holding the template firmly.

2 Get the children to cover the shape with white glue or a glue pen.

3 Sprinkle some sand on top. Shake off the excess. (Some adult supervision is needed here.) As they work, chat about where a camel usually lives (if not in a zoo), and what makes it such an unusual animal. Imagine what it would be like to travel across the desert like Abraham and his family. They would see sand everywhere and feel it blowing all around them.

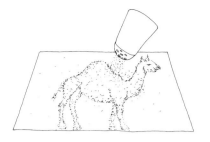

4 Draw a stripe 2–3 cm long at the bottom of the pictures. Encourage the children to fill in the space with glue and repeat the sprinkling process.

5 Encourage the children to feel the sand and let it trickle through their fingers. Ask them if they can count how many grains of sand there are in their hands or on their camel pictures. Remind them of God's promise that one day Abraham would have more people in his family

than there are grains of sand on the beach. Amazing!

6 This activity can be used for several Bible stories including: a wife for Isaac (Genesis 24:1–67) or Joseph going to Egypt (Genesis 37:12–36).

(TIP) *Use flat craft sticks ('lolly' sticks) if you run out of glue spreaders.*

You can find a template of a camel on page 83.

It was a long journey to the new land, but Abraham knew God had promised to be with him.

---

1 Make crowns for each child with the strips of metallic card. Cut a decorative pattern along the top edge of each one. Or, get the children to draw with glue along the top edge and dip the crown in glitter.

2 Encourage the children to draw up to five jewel shapes on each crown using the templates.

3 Get them to spread glue on one jewel shape at a time, and then cover it with

glitter, cellophane or scrunched-up tissue paper. As the children work, talk about Queen Esther and how she was married to the king of a very great country. Explain that a crown is part of a king or queen's uniform so that everybody knows who they are and the important job they do. Esther did something very important.

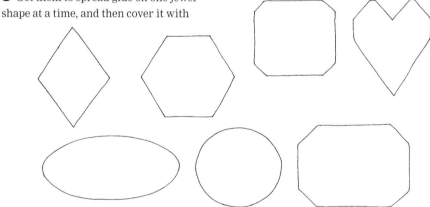

God's people were in danger and Esther saved them. God helped her to be brave.

4 When the crowns are complete, leave them to dry for a few minutes. Wrap each crown around the owner's head and adjust to the correct size. Secure with tape or grips.

5 Encourage the children to wear their crowns and remember that God thinks they are very special and important.

(TIP) *Use this activity with any Bible story about kings or queens, such as Saul, David, Solomon, Jezebel and Josiah.*

Kings and queens are very special people. God thinks you are special, too.

It doesn't matter whether you have lots of money or not. Jesus wants everyone to be part of his family.

Could you share something special you have with a friend?

1 Give each child a sheet of card. Write their name on it.

2 Encourage them to fill it with purple. They should cover areas with glue and stick on purple collage material. Older children might prefer to draw a person wearing robes and use purple fabric and paper to design the clothes rather than making an abstract picture.

3 Explain that, in the part of the world where Jesus lived, only very rich people could afford to wear clothes which were

purple because the dye cost so much money. Lydia sold purple cloth and knew lots of rich people. But Lydia also belonged to Jesus' family, and she was kind to other people. Lydia was happy to share everything she had and invited visitors to stay in her lovely house.

Junk modelling

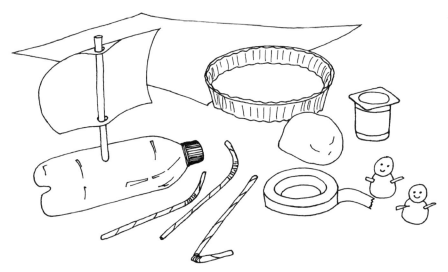

Junk modelling is all about creating models from what other people might consider rubbish! All of your cartons, pots, cardboard tubes and boxes can be used in model-making. Do not throw anything away! But make sure you have enough space to store both the raw materials and, if necessary, the finished products.

Use paper masking tape, with school or white glue, to fix the models in place, as it can be painted or drawn on. Open out cardboard boxes and turn them inside out so that you paint on the plain cardboard rather than the shiny printed side. Reassemble them, with glue or masking tape, before painting. Prepare a model or two to show the children, or sit alongside them and make your own models, but leave them free to create.

If the children are painting the models themselves, they may not be dry enough to take home. Consider painting the boxes yourself beforehand, to avoid this problem, although the models in the activities suggested here do not need to be painted.

The children's creativity is limited only by the materials available and the time provided. So make sure you have lots of junk and allow plenty of time – perhaps more than one session will be needed. Enjoy being creative – and do not worry about the mess!

Children are naturally imaginative. Where we might see an old cardboard box, they can see a bus or a house. As you allow the children to be creative, reflect on how God often sees beyond the surface to the potential. He can turn the unwanted and the ordinary into something worthwhile and valuable. The children are showing something of the creative and recreative genius of their heavenly Father as they model, experiment and play.

Jonah runs away

Making a boat
Jonah 1

15 mins

You will need:
cartons and tubs made of tin foil, plastic or cardboard, modelling clay, sticks and straws, paper, play people, a bowl of water

Jesus in the manger

Making a bed for the baby
Luke 2:1–7

10 mins

You will need:
boxes, tubs and egg carton lids, wooden dolly pegs or chenille wires, scraps of fabric and tissue paper, felt-tip pens, sticky tape, hay or shredded paper

Joseph's clever plan

Build a barn
Genesis 41:46–57

15 mins

You will need:
boxes, cartons and tubs, scissors, glue, sticky tape, oats or cereal flakes, play people, felt-tip pens or paint (optional), cover-up and clean-up equipment

1 Challenge the children to make a boat, using the materials provided. Try not to direct them too much. Ask open-ended questions like: 'Do you think your boat will float?' 'What would be the best materials to use?' 'How could you make a sail?' 'How many play people can fit into your boat?'

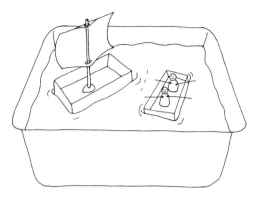

2 As you play alongside the children, tell them about a man, called Jonah. Say: 'God wanted him to go to a city called Nineveh and tell people about him. But Jonah didn't want to go. He ran away and jumped on a boat going in the opposite direction.'

3 Test out the finished boats in the water and add some play people. Say: 'God was angry with Jonah. He sent a big storm.'

4 Encourage the children to disturb the water with their hands to make a storm.

Why do you think God sent the storm?

Can you find out what happened next?

Ask: 'Do the boats still stay afloat?' Say: 'Jonah knew the storm was his fault. He knew the storm would stop if he wasn't in the boat, so he jumped out.' (*Jump one of the play people out of the boat.*) Say: 'God sent a big fish to rescue Jonah, and the sea became calm again.'

---

1 Talk to the children about babies. Ask them: 'Where do babies usually sleep?', 'Where did you sleep when you were a baby?', 'Why did you sleep in cots and prams?', 'What did you have to keep you warm?'.

2 Tell the children that baby Jesus did not have a cot or a pram when he was born. He had a haybox to sleep in – the

What keeps you warm in bed?

Why was God's Son put in a haybox?

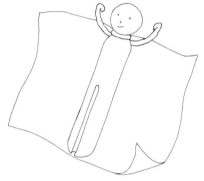

place where the hay was put for the animals to eat! He was wrapped in cloths and kept warm with the hay.

3 Invite the children to make their own 'baby Jesus' figure with the pegs or chenille wires. Get them to draw a face on the peg or bend the wire into a person and

then wrap their figure in cloths.

4 Now, can they make the haybox or manger for him to sleep in? What would be the best things to use? How can they make 'baby Jesus' warm? What a surprising place it was for a baby – especially one as wonderful as God's Son!

---

1 Say: 'God had chosen Joseph to do a special job. When the food grew well and the harvest was good, Joseph had to save some of the food. He stored it in great big barns. Then, when there was not much food, he could share out some of the food he had saved in the barns.'

2 Ask the children to make some barns to store food in from the materials available. Explain that the barns need to be big and strong. They need to have a door to take the food in and out. But the door must shut tightly to keep out the rain and rats. Ask the children to consider whether the barns need windows or ramps.

3 Show the children the junk materials and let them construct the barns however they like. If you want, you can provide paints or felt-tip pens to decorate them further.

4 When they have finished, see how much cereal or oats can be stored in them. Would they be safe from rain and rats? Then share out some of the food to your play people, as Joseph would have done.

Was this a good way to share out the food?

Did you have any problems making your barn?

Mobiles

Children love to have hanging decorations in their bedrooms, and will enjoy making these mobiles. This is often an individual activity, but making one together in a group can be fun too, if you have somewhere suitable to hang it.

Make sure you have plenty of adult help when making mobiles. Try to avoid making ones that need to have everything tied on. Threading or using sticky tape is easier and, even then, only the older and more capable children in your group may be able to manage this for themselves. Prepare coat hangers with string tied to them before the session. Get the children to decorate the elements to hang from the mobile and then sit with them to fix the pieces onto a prepared hanger. The children will enjoy seeing the finished product come together.

- Coat hangers make cheap and easy frames to hang strings of all sorts of items: card shapes, shells, dried clay pieces.

- Plant sticks can be used for individual mobiles and garden canes for group ones. Hoops can also be used for group mobiles and can be hung vertically or horizontally. A large central figure or shape inside a decorated hoop is particularly effective.

- Keep the items on mobiles as lightweight as possible so that they turn in any movement of air. Using shiny materials will help them catch the light too.

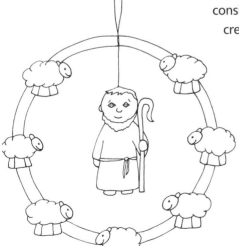

- Something bright, shiny and turning in the air can promote a sense of wonder, so consider making mobiles as part of a creation series.

- Make the characters from a Bible story and hang them from a group mobile. Ask each child to say what happened to their character in the story.

A reminder of the Bible story
Daniel 6

15 mins

You will need:
short plant sticks, 30 cm lengths of wool, yellow card circles and triangles, yellow wool (2 cm lengths), a simple card picture of Daniel

A message for the shepherds

A way to celebrate
Luke 2:8–20

15 mins

You will need:
gold or silver string, geometric card shapes in bright and shiny colours, a fine knitting needle, some 1 cm lengths of brightly coloured drinking straws, pictures of Jesus in the manger (drawn onto card or cut from Christmas cards)

Jesus and the children

A group activity
Mark 10:13–16

15 mins

You will need:
cut-out people shapes (one for each child), a 'Jesus' figure (in the same proportions as the people shapes), a hoop, wool, collage materials (optional), a large mirror (optional)

1 Tell the children about brave Daniel who loved God and always prayed to him three times a day. Say: 'Daniel worked for a king. This king listened to men who did not like Daniel. They persuaded him to make a law saying that no one should pray to anyone, except him. The punishment was to be put into the place where the lions lived. When the king heard that Daniel always prayed to God and so would have to be put in the lions' pit, he realised how silly he had been. But he found out how great God is, because God kept

Daniel safe all the time he was with the lions.'

2 Give out the pictures of Daniel and get the children to colour in Daniel, back and front.

3 Help each child to make at least two lions. Give everyone a circle of card and get them to stick a fringe of yellow wool around it and draw the lion's face in the centre. Fix the circle to a point on a triangle of card.

4 Put short lengths of sticky tape along a table edge for the children to pick up easily. Help them to fix wool to each

character and to the plant stick, putting Daniel in the centre.

5 Hang the mobile by one length of wool tied to both ends of the stick.

Wasn't God great to keep Daniel safe?

What do you talk to God about?

---

1 Before the session, cut a 50 cm length of string for each child and knot a hanging loop at one end. Make a small hole in each card shape using the knitting needle.

 Do not use a hole punch as the holes will be too big; the straws will slip through.

2 Tell the story about the shepherds on the hills outside Bethlehem: 'An angel appeared one night to some shepherds on the hills outside Bethlehem. They had some amazing news about the baby born in the town. He was the person promised by God long ago. The shepherds would

know they had found the right baby because they would find him wrapped up and lying in the animals' food box. After the angel had spoken to them, the shepherds heard lots more angels singing songs of praise to God. Then they went to Bethlehem and found the baby Jesus.'

What did the shepherds do when they heard about Jesus?

What can you sing to praise God?

3 Tell the children they are going to make a hanging decoration to remind them of the angel's message to the shepherds. Encourage them to thread alternate cards and straws on to the string. Help them to fix a picture of Jesus (see page 81) to the end of the string with sticky tape.

---

1 Before the session, cut out people shapes and write a child's name on the back of each one. Make one for each of the children.

2 In the session, give out the people shapes to the correct children and ask them to decorate these to make pictures of themselves. Suggest they look in the mirror to check details. Children who finish early can help decorate the 'Jesus' figure.

3 Hold up 'Jesus'. Say: 'Some children in Bible times wanted to meet Jesus. Their parents tried to take them to see him. (*Ask the children to hold their figures facing 'Jesus'.*) Jesus' friends tried to stop them.

(*Get them to turn their figures away.*) But Jesus said he wanted to see the children. (*Tell them to turn their figures to face 'Jesus' again.*) He gave them hugs and asked God to bless them.'

4 Say that Jesus loves children today too and wants God to bless them. The mobile you will make together will remind everyone of this.

5 Fix equal lengths of wool to the children's figures with sticky tape and arrange them around the hoop. Tie two pieces of yarn across the hoop and hang the 'Jesus' figure from where they cross. This should be at about the same height as the children's figures when the hoop is hung up.

6 Take turns to say thank you to Jesus for loving each person.

What would you say if you met Jesus?

Thank Jesus for loving you!

Models

When making structured models, the children are given specific instructions to follow or another model to copy, rather than using their own ideas from a selection of materials. Models of this sort can be helpful in the understanding and retelling of Bible stories, as well as giving the children the satisfaction of having something to display.

Model making can be a combined or individual effort. If you make one as a group, make sure that every child participates and that they see the model in use. Individual models should, of course, be taken home.

- Collect boxes, tubes and packaging as an ongoing activity so that you always have plenty to use. Small boxes (for jellies or snack portions of raisins) are especially useful.

- Check what your group has planned to do in the future and bear this in mind as you save junk.

- Put a container at church for other people to collect items for you. Keep them informed of particular needs.

- When making models, you will need a high ratio of adults to children as, at some time, they will each need one-to-one help.

- Strong glue may be needed to fix some items together. Sticky tape may be more useful.

- Use masking tape as an alternative fixing agent. It is easy to tear and can be coloured with felt-tip pens or paint. However, it is not meant to be strongly adhesive so it is not suitable for a 'permanent' model.

- Remember that models may need time to dry or stick. Put them in a suitable place, out of reach. Making them on trays may help here!

- Allow time for the children to retell a story using the model after they have heard it. Ask questions to help them: 'What happened next?', 'Who were the people in the story?', 'What did God do?'

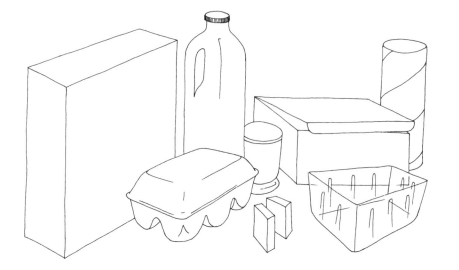

Crossing the Red Sea

A 'working model'
Exodus 14:1–29

15 mins

You will need:
two A2 sheets of blue card, blue, green and transparent collage materials, sticky tape, small rectangles of white card, modelling clay or Blu-tack

What did God do that was so amazing?

What would you have said to God?

A home for Elisha

A simple play house
2 Kings 4:8–10

15–20 mins

You will need:
a shoebox or similar for each child, small boxes, card and collage scraps, pictures of an oil lamp, modelling clay (optional)

Jesus heals a blind man

An unusual way to 'see' what Jesus did
Luke 18:35–43

15 mins

You will need:
two paper plates for each child, split pin paper fasteners, plate-sized semicircles of dark paper to fit into the centre of the plates, wool for hair, glue

1 Cut one sheet of card in half. Let the children decorate each half with collage materials to make the sea.

2 Tape the two pieces of 'sea' on top of the whole sheet at the opposite ends. Make sure you can lift up the middle flaps.

3 Ask the children to draw a person on each small rectangle. (Do not worry about clear representations!) Cut around the people roughly and stand them in blobs of modelling clay or Blu-tack.

4 Say: 'God's people were escaping from their enemies. They had reached the edge of the sea. (*Put all the people by the edge of the sea.*) The people knew their enemies were not far behind. They were

frightened. "Don't worry!" said Moses, their leader. "God will save us." Moses held out his hand over the sea. God sent a strong wind and it blew the sea back. (*Open each side of the 'sea' so that it stands on each side.*) The ground dried up to make a path. Moses and the people walked across. (*Move the people between the 'sea'.*) Then the sea came back together behind them. (*Fold the 'sea' flat again.*) God had saved them!'

---

1 Say: 'There once was a rich woman who lived in a big house. Elisha was one of God's messengers. He travelled around the countryside and often visited the woman and her husband. One day the woman decided she wanted to do something special for Elisha. She would give him his own room to stay in. It would be on the roof, as houses in that country had flat roofs. She would put a bed, a table,

a chair and a lamp in the room. "Elisha can stay in the room whenever he visits us," said the woman.'

2 Ask the children to imagine they are the woman making the room comfortable for Elisha. Help them to make simple furniture with small boxes, or draw the items on cards and glue to the sides of boxes. Give out the lamp pictures and get the children to colour them or you can encourage them to make lamps with modelling clay.

3 Give out the shoeboxes. Cut out doors and windows at the children's request, but let them arrange the furniture.

4 Say that Elisha was very grateful for

his room, and later was able to help the woman in amazing ways. God was very good to all of them!

How was the woman kind to Elisha?

Say thank you to God for something he has given you.

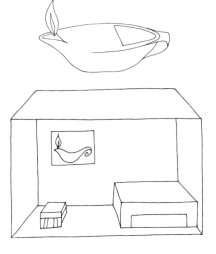

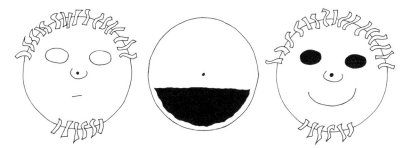

1 Before the session, make a small hole (for the fasteners) in the centre of each plate. Draw eye shapes on half of the plates and cut round holes inside them. Draw small straight lines for the mouths.

2 Give each child a plate with eyeholes and let them glue 'hair' around the edge. They should glue the dark semicircle onto the second plate.

3 Fasten the two plates together with a split pin, with the face on the top. Make sure the plates are turned so that the eyeholes are blank.

4 Tell the children about the blind man who sat at the side of the road: 'He was sad because he could not see anything. His eyes did not work properly. But he could hear, and when he heard Jesus

coming along, he shouted out for help. Jesus asked what he wanted and he said that he wanted to see. Jesus made his eyes work properly and he was able to see again. (*At this point, ask the children to turn the bottom plate until the 'eyes' show through the holes.*) He followed along with Jesus, thanking God all the time.' (*Ask the children to turn the man's mouth into a smile.*)

Why did the man say thank you to God?

Say thank you to God for something you can see.

Montage

Montage is a technique in which fragments of pictures and words are combined to make a new whole picture. It is an interesting and useful art form for making posters and banners, especially on a particular theme.

The idea is to completely cover a background with a selection of small pictures, overlapping them slightly, and to include some appropriate words. For very young children, only use a few words which they will easily understand. For instance, give each child a house-shaped piece of paper, with the words 'Home', 'Family' and their name written on it, and ask them to add pictures which remind them of their own home and the people who live there. Pictures of furniture, food and toys can be easily found in catalogues and magazines. Pictures labelled 'My day out' or 'On the way' could include postcards, promotional leaflets for days out, and photographs.

● If you are working on a large picture, all together, several children can add pictures at one time. It does not matter where individual pictures are placed, or whether they are put on straight – as long as they are the correct way up. It is the all-over effect that counts. It is, however, important that an adult supervises the gluing process, makes sure gaps are filled, and helps in the positioning of words.

● If you are making a poster, use thin card or heavy quality paper as it will be quite heavy when glued and could easily tear while it is wet.

● Suitable pictures can also be cut (or torn) from advertisements and used greetings cards. Some 3- to 4-year-olds may like to cut out their own, but make sure they use safety scissors.

● Montage is ideal as a basis for discussion. It encourages children to think about their understanding and experiences of a particular theme. Their ideas can then be developed and linked with the Bible topic. Children will enjoy comparing Jesus' life as a child in Nazareth with their own experiences of home life in the twenty-first century. Or, you could link your montage about journeys, with stories about Abraham, Moses or the Good Samaritan. Talk about how these people would have travelled. Which method would the children prefer?

Let's praise God

A group poster
Psalm 150

15 mins

You will need:
sheets of A2 card, photocopies of a few favourite praise songs and chants, pictures of musical instruments and musicians, musical note-shapes cut from coloured paper, 'Let's praise God' written in large lettering, white glue

God makes the light and sky

A day and night picture
Genesis 1:1–8,14–19

15 mins

You will need:
sheets of white card or one large sheet, black paper, individual pictures of stars, the sun, the moon, cloud shapes, a rainbow, lightning, sky-coloured paper (cut from advertisements in newspaper supplements), star stickers, silver glitter (optional), the words 'light', 'sky' 'day' and 'night' (written or typed)

Noah and the big flood

Build a boat with Noah
Genesis 7:1–8,12

15 mins

You will need:
a large boat shape cut from stiff brown paper, pictures of different animals, dove and raven shapes, blue and green paper, wavy patterned scissors, white glue, a black marker pen, drawings of Noah and his family

1 Work with a maximum of four children at a time, but make sure every child has an opportunity to choose at least one picture to stick on.

2 Cut or tear the copies of praise songs and chants into several large pieces. Glue these randomly at angles across the background card and overlap them so there are few gaps.

3 Add the words of one or two favourite praise chants, some musical symbols, pictures of musical instruments and musicians on top of the musical background, allowing some of it to show through. Include some pictures of percussion instruments, if possible the same as the ones your group uses to accompany their songs. As the children work on the montage, chat about their favourite musical instruments, praise songs and rhymes. Choose a song to sing together.

4 Attach the words 'Let's praise God!' onto the poster and explain that there are lots of different ways we can praise God – by singing, playing instruments, clapping and dancing.

Turn to pages 48 and 49 for ideas for making your own musical instruments.

 Look on the Internet for free music clipart to download.
Find over 200 rhymes and songs in Tiddlywinks: Say and Sing.

Look for the different ways people praise God at your church.

---

1 Help each child to cover half of their background sheet with black paper to represent night time. Get them to cover the other half with a selection of sky colours.

2 Chat about the sky, light and darkness. Take the children outside to see what the sky looks like today, or look out of the window. Does it change?

3 Ask the children to choose some of the other pictures to glue onto the background. Ask: 'Which ones can we see in the daytime and which in the night-time?' Clouds could be pasted across the joins. Encourage them to draw raindrops or snowflakes falling.

4 Read Genesis 1:16,17 from a contemporary version of the Bible. Ask the children what the big lights God made are called.

5 Add stars and glitter to the night side. Complete the montage by adding the words where the children think they should go.

 Very young children might find star stickers too fiddly. You could use metallic confetti stars instead.

Go outside with a grown-up. Look up at the sky. Watch the clouds moving. Can you see either of the big lights God made?

---

1 Work in groups of four children at a time, with adult supervision.

2 Draw lines to show where the bottom part of the boat and the roof areas are. Encourage the children to fill the middle section completely with pictures of animals, preferably two of each, and glue birds onto the roof.

3 Cut some strips from the blue and green paper, using the wavy patterned scissors. Get the children to glue them at random onto the lower part of the boat so that the waves extend beyond the boat at both ends.

4 Cut out some doors and windows. Fix these onto the boat so the animals can still be seen. Add drawings of Noah and his family and the title, 'Noah and the big flood'.

5 Get the children to think about being on the boat. Ask them: 'What would it

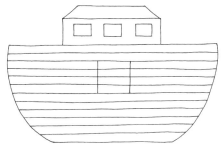

have been like to live on the boat with all those animals?', 'Would it have been noisy, smelly, hardly room to move?', 'What about feeding time?'

6 Look at the completed montage together. Encourage the children to name the animals. Try making lots of different animal sounds together to imagine what the noise level on the boat would have been like!

 *God promised to keep Noah and his family safe – and he did! He looks after you, too.*

Mosaic

Mosaic is an old technique originally used to produce a pattern or picture by arranging small, variously coloured pieces of glass, stone or tiles onto a firm base. The Romans, in particular, used this technique for flooring.

This idea can be adapted by using squares of paper in a variety of colours and gluing them onto a background. Use squares that measure at least 3 cm as anything smaller will be difficult for young children to handle.

The simplest method is to provide a choice of coloured paper squares for the children to stick at random onto background paper to make an abstract picture. Alternatively, you could use a paper plate or a base from food packaging as the background.

You could draw an outline on a sheet of paper for the children to fill with mosaic patterns. They could add details with felt-tip pens when the design is complete.

Cut out a shape, such as animals, from card and encourage the children to cover it in mosaic. Trim it later to remove paper that has gone over the edges.

There are lots of different kinds of paper you can use, but try to find ones which are a similar thickness if you are using them for filling in an outline shape. You could use: tissue paper, wrapping paper, advertisements from leaflets, magazines or newspaper supplements or used coloured envelopes. Gummed paper is more expensive but very good because the colours are bold and the surface is shiny. It is better however, to use white glue rather than licking the back of each square.

Work with small groups of children and have adult help to supervise gluing and stop the children throwing paper all over the floor.

Mosaic is a very effective art technique and encourages children to be creative as they discover that different combinations of colour make interesting patterns. Decorating animal shapes could help children to think about the variety of patterns and colours of animal fur that God has created. Be imaginative and have fun!

Joseph's coat

Joseph and his brothers
Genesis 37:1–11

15–20 mins

You will need:
a length of lining paper or wallpaper, lots of large coloured squares, white glue, thick black marker pens, crayons, pencils

God makes animals

All kinds of animals
Genesis 1:20 – 2:4

5–8* mins

You will need:
cut-out shapes of different animals; plain paper squares (3 cm²) cut from magazines in browns, greys, white and black; white glue; scissors

*time per animal

Bread for everyone

Loaves and fish
John 6:1–14

15 mins

You will need:
a large paper plate or circle of card for each child; two large fish shapes cut from card per child; brown paper circles (five per child); 3 cm x 3 cm paper squares in grey, silver, light brown and beige tones; self-adhesive spots for eyes; white glue; scissors

1 Four children could work on this activity at one time, with adult supervision. (Two children on each side.)

2 Put the length of lining paper on the floor, securing the corners with masking tape, if necessary. Ask a child to lie on top of the paper and keep very still, while you pencil around them. When the shape is completed, draw the outline of a long robe onto it.

3 Explain that Jacob loved his son Joseph very much, so he gave him a very special coat as a present. Now you are all going to work together to make a really beautiful picture of Joseph

wearing that coat. Spread glue over one or two sections of the robe at a time. Show the children how to stick on the paper squares to make a patchwork pattern.

4 When the whole of the robe is filled in, use crayons to draw Joseph's facial features and hair.

  *Put the mosaic squares into several boxes or baskets. That way, if a container is dropped, there will be less to clear up.*
Using a few richly patterned or metallic squares cut from gift wrap makes the coat look really special.

What are you wearing today?
Does God only love you when you wear special clothes?

---

1 One adult can supervise about five children for this activity.

2 Give each child an animal shape. Provide lots of paper squares in white, black, and various shades of brown and grey. Encourage the children to cover the shape with glue and then completely cover it with the coloured paper. Very young children will probably just like to glue on a few squares randomly rather than trying to make a neat mosaic pattern.

3 Talk about some of the animals God has made, the different colours and interesting patterns on their fur or skin. Chat about tigers, giraffes, leopards, zebras – their stripes, patches and spots. Can you make the sound each animal makes? Challenge the children to think of a colour and then name some animals with that colour.

4 When the mosaic has dried a little, trim the edges to neaten them.

5 Ask the children to hold up their animal shapes. Admire them and say a

'thank you' prayer for all the amazing variety of animals God has made to live in his world.

 Let the children use their creativity and imagination to make their animals as varied and colourful as they wish.

What animals do you like best?
Say thank you to God for them.

---

1 You will need one adult to supervise each group of between four and six children, for this activity. Give each child two fish shapes and help them to decorate it with silver and grey mosaic squares. Put on spots for the eyes.

2 Encourage them to decorate the edge of the circle or plate with brown squares to make a basket. Tell the story of the young boy who gave his lunch to Jesus – and how Jesus used one little meal of bread and fish to feed lots and lots of people.

3 Give out five brown circles (bread roll shapes) to each child to complete the boy's meal.

4 As the children work, talk about the care the boy's mummy took in preparing his picnic, and how he must have been very hungry by the end of the day.

Comment that it was really kind of him to share his meal when he needed it to eat it himself.

5 When everyone has finished, ask the children to hold them while you say a prayer, thanking God for providing us with good food to eat.

 *Think about people in countries where there is not enough food. Are there any ways the children think we can help them?*

The boy was very kind to share his meal. How could you be kind to someone?

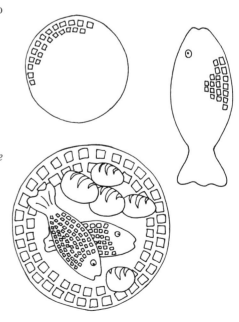

Mural or frieze

A mural or frieze is an opportunity for large scale production with a group of children. As well as brightening up a dull spot on your walls, friezes and murals can be a good way of involving the children in telling the Bible story, and reminding them of it in the future. Friezes can give children the opportunity to tell others about the story or topic.

Say to the children, before you begin, that this is a 'together activity' for everyone to enjoy, so they will not be taking anything home this time. During the activity, point out to each of them how important their individual part is to the whole design.

Before you start, think about these issues:

● Plan where your mural or frieze will be displayed and how large it will be. Cut backing paper or card to this size.

● Plan what will be on your frieze. The background will need to be prepared first. You could paint it (remember, paint may take some time to dry), draw or glue things on, or leave it plain. The children will be eager to put their contributions anywhere so work out in advance where you want each element.

● Include different techniques when making your frieze. Some parts could be painted while others are printed, collaged, cut from rubbings, or drawn with crayons, felt-tip pens or chalks.

● Use different materials and textures, perhaps using fabric, cards of different thicknesses and wallpaper. Add details such as hair (wool), real leaves, or feathers.

● Make your frieze three dimensional by using sticky foam pads or even small flat boxes to bring the important things forward. Add extra interest by using smells – spices or dried herbs on food pictures or perfume on flowers or blossoms!

● On a fine day, get the children to 'paint' a frieze with water on an outside wall. Your frieze will not last, of course, but the children will love doing it!

What do you think is the best thing about God's city?

What will you say to God when you meet him there?

A tiny seed

A story Jesus told
Matthew 13:31,32

15 mins

You will need:
a sheet of light brown card for the background, potting compost, a large seed or an oval sheet of coloured paper, brown and green paper strips, leaves (see point 4), pictures of birds (from magazines, greetings cards or children's drawings), shredded brown tissue paper, glue, cover-up and clean-up equipment

God the Maker

A scene to inspire praise
Psalm 104

15–20 mins

You will need:
plain backing paper, thick green and blue paint, combs, green tissue paper, coloured and animal print paper, shiny paper

The city of God

A BIG picture
Revelation 21,22

15–20 mins

You will need:
backing paper with river marked, building and tree shapes from gold card, shiny scraps in various colours, clear or blue shredded cellophane, sticky foam pads, tissue paper, large round sequins, long boxes, such as toothpaste boxes

1 Spread glue across the lower quarter of the background card. Sprinkle on compost, press down lightly, and then shake off the excess. Say that this is going to be your field.

2 Pretend to be the farmer in the story Jesus told and plant a seed in your field. (Glue the seed onto your picture.) What will happen now?

3 Get the children to add paper strips, one by one, to make the first growth, and then the trunk and branches of a tree.

4 Help them to make leaves. They could: make handprints with green paint and cut them out; print using real leaves; make rubbings of leaves; or use real dried leaves. You could use all four methods. Give your tree a leafy top.

5 Read Matthew 13:31,32. Look in your Bible and find that Jesus said that birds came and nested in the tree. Get everyone to stick shredded tissue paper to the frieze in clumps to make nests. Make birds to live in them.

6 Say that Jesus told this story to show that God's family keeps growing and growing.

(TIP) For a 3-D version of this activity, stand a twiggy branch in a pot of firm sand. Hang leaves on this 'tree' and add a nest and some birds.

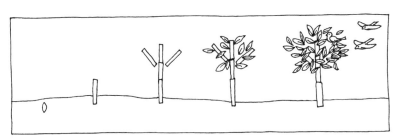

We can be part of God's family too.

Do you know any other stories Jesus told?

---

1 Tell the children that everyone is going to make a frieze all about God and the wonderful world he has made.

2 Draw a sloping line on the background to indicate a hilly horizon. Include a section that will be the sea. Let the children paint the earth and sea with the thick paint and comb patterns in it to add texture. Leave this to dry.

3 Say: 'Listen! This is what our great God has made!' Read out some of the verses from Psalm 104, such as verses 10–12,17,18,21 and 25.

4 Talk about the different plants, animals and sea creatures. Make some trees together using small pieces of tissue

paper. Then suggest that the children choose an animal or sea creature to make. Show them the animal print and shiny paper to stimulate their ideas.

5 Help the children decide where to place their creatures. Admire each one individually, with some remark such as, 'Wasn't God clever to think of making lions?'

6 Look at your frieze together as you read out verses 24 and 25 from Psalm 104.

Have a selection of body, head and leg shapes so the children can make animals quickly.

What do you think is the best thing God has made?

What will you say to praise God?

1 Tell the children that you are going to be thinking about the wonderful city that God is preparing for us in heaven. The Bible tells us that the city is very beautiful. It is made of gold and decorated with shiny precious jewels. Read Revelation 21:11 and 18, saying 'jewel' instead of 'jasper'.

2 Give out the building shapes and let the children decorate them with shiny 'jewels'. Fix these buildings along the edge of the river, with the smaller ones in the distance. Use foam pads under the foreground buildings to give a further sense of perspective.

3 Tell the children that a beautiful river flows through God's city. Read Revelation 22:1,2a. Let the children help you glue the shredded cellophane along the line of the river.

4 Say that beautiful fruit trees grow beside the river. Read out Revelation 22:2b. Help the children glue tissue paper leaves and sequin fruits to the treetops. Make the trees stand forward by gluing the long boxes under them.

5 Look at the picture together and talk about God's beautiful city.

Musical instruments

Children love playing musical instruments and discovering the different sounds they can make. Sounds can be made in several different ways including shaking, banging, blowing and scraping. Sounds can also be made with various body parts.

Allow the children to play with different instruments. Can they play loudly and softly, quickly and slowly? Can they copy a pattern or rhythm? Can they play in time with the rhythm of some music? It is even more fun when the children have made their own instruments. In this section, there are ideas for making simple instruments and using them in different ways.

Playing instruments is something that everyone can join in with together. You don't have to be musical – all ages and abilities can play together and enjoy being part of a group. Playing instruments together can help physical coordination, discipline and self-control as well as it being fun and therapeutic.

Jesus calms a storm

Story with shakers
Mark 4:35–41

15 mins

You will need:
plastic cups or yoghurt pots (two per child or group), sticky tape, collage scraps and glue, dried peas, rice or pasta

Joshua and the battle of Jericho

Making trumpets
Joshua 6:1–20

10–15 mins

You will need:
cardboard tubes, disposable cups, sticky tape, scissors, card, cardboard boxes, bricks or kneelers

Praising God

Tambourines and cymbals
Psalm 150

15 mins

You will need:
foil circles such as milk bottle tops or small pie cases, a shoelace or a large bodkin with string for each child, a lump of play dough, modelling clay or Blu-tack, pan lids, trumpets (see above)

1 Tell the children you are going to make a shaker.

2 Help the children to fill one of the cups with dried peas, rice or pasta and fasten the other one on top using sticky tape. Get everyone to experiment with different fillings and different amounts. What different sounds do they make?

3 Encourage everyone to decorate their shaker with collage scraps.

4 When they have finished, ask the children to practise shaking their shakers gently to make a quiet sound or hard to make a loud sound. If you have used different fillings, try ordering them from quietest to loudest.

5 Tell the story of Jesus calming the storm. Say: 'Jesus' friends were all very frightened as the storm grew. It didn't help that Jesus was asleep! (*Encourage the children to make a quiet sound and build up to a crescendo. You could do this by gradually shaking harder; starting with*

one shaker and then adding more; or starting with the rice shakers and then the pasta ones.) Jesus woke up and said to the storm, "Be still!" (*Encourage the children to stop playing suddenly*.) Even the wind and waves did what he said!'

 Try other fillings such as instant coffee granules, sugar, paper clips, coins and gravel.

Who can keep you safe in a storm?
Could you stop a storm from storming?

1 Before the session, cut off the bottom of each cup.

2 Give each child a cup and a cardboard tube. Show them how to fasten the bottom of the cup to the tube with the sticky tape, to make a trumpet. Alternatively, you could roll some card into a cone or cylinder shape and fasten with sticky tape. Practise blowing loudly!

3 Say: 'God told his friend, Joshua, to use some trumpets in a very special way. The trumpets would help God's people get to a special place. God told Joshua and the

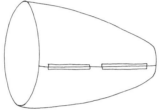

people to march round the city of Jericho for a week. On the seventh day, they had to shout and blow their trumpets.'

4 Suggest that together you do what Joshua did. First, build the walls of the city with the boxes, bricks or kneelers. March round the boxes seven times, counting as you go. Then blow the trumpets loudly and shout.

5 Ask: 'Do you know what happened next?' Say: 'God made the walls of the city come crashing down!' Knock over the 'walls' with the children. Say: 'Now the people could get into the new land God had promised them.'

Who made the walls fall down?
Can you blow your trumpet to praise God?

---

1 Give each child at least eight foil circles and help them to thread them onto the string or shoelace.

2 Tie the ends of the string together to make a tambourine. Encourage them to shake it to make a lovely, silvery sound.

3 Give out the pan lids and encourage the children to bang them together to make cymbals.

4 Help the children to make the trumpets as described in the activity above.

5 Say that for hundreds of years, people have praised and worshipped God with musical instruments, and that you are going to do the same today!

6 Encourage the children to sit in three groups: one with trumpets, one with tambourines and one with cymbals. Alternatively, each child could have one of each. Ask them to listen out for the names of the instruments.

7 *Say*:
'Praise God! God is great! Praise him!
Praise him with the sound of trumpets.
(*Play the trumpets.*)

Praise him with tambourines and dancing.
(*Shake the tambourines and dance.*)

Praise him with the clash of cymbals.
(*Bang the cymbals together.*)

Let everything praise God! Praise God!'

 If you are using a bodkin, show the children how to push it through the foil into some dough.

 Teach the children a sign for 'Stop!' before they start playing their instruments.

Can you make a happy sound?
How do you want to praise God?

Natural objects

Discovering different materials and textures from the natural world can be a wonderful way to help children appreciate God's creativity. Allow them time to explore the objects as well as to use them in the activity.

Be aware of safety issues. Never use anything that is sharp or poisonous. Always remind the children not to put any of the objects in their mouths and to wash their hands after handling them.

● Get the children to help you collect objects, for instance, in autumn or on the beach. You will need to have plenty of supervision and be particularly careful that the children do not pick up unsuitable items. They will enjoy using what they collected later.

● Do not try to include every natural object in one activity. Choose items with care, linking them, if possible, to the story or Bible passage. Suggested objects include: fir cones, bark, twigs, leaves, rose hips, conkers, seeds, corn, grasses, feathers, sheep's wool, sand, shells, stones, wood shavings, vegetables.

● Leaves will dry out, curl up and become brittle very quickly. Flatten them while they are still soft by putting them between sheets of newspaper and under heavy books for a few days. This will keep their shape.

● Print with leaves or vegetables. Have plenty of items so that a clean leaf or vegetable can be used with each new colour. Put paint on a plate rather than in a pot so the children can dip the items in easily.

● Natural objects are often heavy, so attach them to strong card.

● In many instances you may need extra strong glue. Be aware that some glues should be used by adults only, but the children can indicate where it is needed. Warn the children that some items may take a while to stick firmly.

God feeds Elijah

A scene from the story
1 Kings 17:1–7

You will need:
a strong backing sheet, crayons, dried grasses, twigs, black feathers, a bird-shaped card for each child, joggle eyes, a picture of Elijah, sticky foam pads, small squares of dry toast

Simeon and Anna

Making characters from a Bible story
Luke 2:22–38

You will need:
sheets of A4 card in autumn colours, 15 cm circles of skin-tone card, autumn collectibles such as conkers, seeds, leaves, sheep's wool or old man's beard (wild clematis)

The two houses

Exploring textures and how things work
Matthew 7:24–27

You will need:
sheets of A4 backing card for individual pictures (or an A2 sheet for a group picture), small card squares, soft dry sand, small stones, one large stone

1 Tell the children: 'There was going to be a time when no rain would fall and everything would get all dried up. God wanted to look after his friend, Elijah. (*Show the picture.*) So this is what he did.' Read the story from 1 Kings 17:2–6 or tell it in your own words.

2 Draw a stream across the backing sheet with a blue crayon. Get the children to stick the grass and twigs on to make the countryside. Talk about how everything is very dry because no rain has fallen.

3 Give out the bird-shaped card and encourage the children to colour the beaks with crayon and glue the feathers to the bodies. Glue a joggle eye on each finished bird.

4 Put the picture together using foam pads under Elijah and the birds.

5 Remind the children of how God sent the birds with food for Elijah. Glue a square of toast to each bird's beak.

 *Make extra birds so that the children can take their own home to remind them of God's care.*

How did God look after Elijah?

How does God look after you?

---

1 If possible, arrange for the children to help you collect the objects.

2 Talk about the objects and their colours. Mention that, although the trees are losing their leaves and getting ready for winter, for some of them it is their most beautiful time of year. Say that Simeon and Anna in our story were older people, but their old age was the best time for them because they met Jesus then.

3 Tell the children about Mary and Joseph bringing baby Jesus to God's Temple building. Say: 'There they met an old man called Simeon. He cuddled baby Jesus and sang a song about him. Simeon knew the baby was God's promised person. Mary and Joseph also met Anna. She was a very old lady who loved to worship God in the temple. She thanked God for Jesus and told everyone how important Jesus was.'

4 Give every child a sheet of card and help them to glue a card circle in the centre. Encourage them to arrange the collectibles to make Anna's or Simeon's faces. Get them to use the sheep's wool or old man's beard for white hair, and glue the objects in place.

5 Admire everyone's picture and say a prayer for the older people you know.

Which older people do you know?

Thank God for them!

---

1 Tell the children that Jesus told a story about two men who built houses. Say: 'One man found a sandy place where it was easy to dig. (*Pass round the sand in a container, encouraging the children to run it through their fingers and feel how soft it is.*)

The second man decided to build his house on a rock. He knew it would be hard work, but it would be strong and firm. (*Pass round the large stone so the children can feel how hard it is.*)

When the houses were built, rain poured down and floods came. The house on the rock was firm and strong. But the sand was washed away so the other house fell down.'

2 Draw some horizon lines across the backing card. Get the children to glue below the lines. Help them to sprinkle sand on the left hand side and arrange the small stones on the right. Encourage them to draw raindrops in the sky.

3 Get the children to arrange the squares to make a house standing on the stony

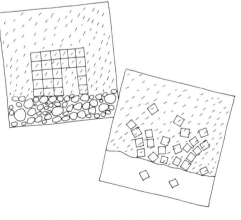

ground and broken down walls on the sand.

4 Say: 'Jesus said that, if we listen to him, we will be wise like the man who built his house on the rock.'

What do you like building?

Ask Jesus to help you listen to him.

2 Making truffles

Try making these delicious sweets. They make a great Mothering Sunday present or you can give them to anyone on a 'Thank-you-for-being-special' occasion!

Be aware of nut allergies! Wash your hands. Make sure everything is clean.

You will need

55 g cream or curd cheese

55 g chopped nuts or dried fruit

55 g icing sugar

30 g cocoa power

about 12 paper or foil sweet cases

a plate for each child

foodwrap

For the coatings:

cocoa powder, desiccated coconut, vermicelli, and hundreds and thousands or sugar strands. Put them out in separate small containers.

What you do

1 Mix the cheese, nuts or fruit, sugar and cocoa together well.

2 Roll the mixture into small balls. Then drop each ball into one of the coatings and roll it round in the container.

3 Put them in the paper cases and place them on a plate. Decorate, for the person who will receive the gift. Cover with food wrap.

Painting with brushes

Painting gives young children great satisfaction – one sweep of the arm leaves a trail of fabulous colour.

Make sure you have the equipment set up before the children arrive. Prepare a place for each child, with a container of quality paper (that does not wrinkle up when wet) readily available. Aspiring artists often want to make two or three paintings within a few minutes!

Little fingers need big chunky brushes, with short handles for easy control. Slightly older children will enjoy having a smaller brush available as well, to put in finer details, like facial features or patterns.

Buy good quality water-based paints intended for young children, in either powder or liquid form. (Poor quality paints often produce weak, watery results and unsatisfactory colour mixing.) Red, blue, yellow, black and white will make all the colours you need, although tubs of flesh pink, leaf green and brown are also handy.

Although rather expensive, inks give fabulous results for effects like sky and water. With water added, a little goes a long way – but protective aprons are a must!

Unless you're doing a colour-mixing activity, it is helpful to have a brush in each tub, so that children do not need to wash out brushes every time they want to change colour. Painting is often easiest in a standing position – on low tables or at easels.

Help the children to write their names on the top left hand corner before they start!

Teach the children how to wipe the excess paint off onto the inner edge of the pot and, after painting, to return the brush to the same colour paint. (This needs careful supervision initially.) Ensure that the children hold the brush in a similar way to holding a pencil, so that they can control it. Help the children to learn to pull the brush down the page – not push it away from them (which is difficult to control and causes jaggy edges on the painting).

 It is a good idea for leaders and helpers to practise how to mix colours and control brushes before using paints with children.

Jesus loves children

Self-portraits
Mark 10:13–16

15–20 mins

You will need:
chunky brushes (plus finer ones for facial details), prepared paints in pots (with lids), variety of colours suitable for flesh, hair and eyes, child-safe mirrors, cover-up and clean-up equipment

Sun

Large-scale painting
Psalm 19

10–15 mins

You will need:
very large sheets of white paper (flip-chart size), pots of yellow and orange paint, aprons, washing facilities and towels, masking tape

Jonah and the big fish

Painting from observation
Jonah 1–3

15–20 mins

You will need:
large sheets of paper; large fresh fish intact to examine (or photographs); paint prepared in pots: grey, blue and green (various shades), red and white; chunky brushes, cover-up and clean-up equipment

1 Tell the story of Jesus and the children from Mark 10:13–16. Emphasise that, even though Jesus was tired and busy, he wanted the children to come to him. Say: 'Jesus loves each one of us exactly as we are and wants to spend time with us. Even

though we cannot see him, we can talk with him any time we want to by praying '

2 Encourage the children to look in the mirrors and observe their different features. Discuss the position, shape, size and colour of the mouth, nose, eyes and hair. Encourage the children to touch these as they look in the mirrors. Use positive, describing words such as: 'nose in the middle', 'ears on the side', wavy or straight hair.

3 Encourage each child to paint a self-portrait. Get them to check their details regularly in the mirror.

4 As the children work, remind them

that each one of us is unique and Jesus loves us just as we are.

5 Create a display of the completed portraits with a heading such as: 'Jesus loves us all'.

 Beforehand, prepare paint in different skin tones suitable for the children in your group, by mixing white, a little red and brown paint together.

What do you like best about how you look?

Talk about how God makes each one of us the same but different.

---

1 Before the session, secure large sheets of paper to a wall or easels using masking tape.

2 Talk about how important it is that God made the sun. Explain that the sun is very, very big.

3 Encourage the children to paint very big suns that fill their paper. As this activity does not take a lot of concentration, chat with them as they work, about how important it is that God made the sun. Demonstrate this to help them understand: leave some seedlings in a dark cupboard for a few days before the session and compare these with seedlings left in the light. Use this to help the

children realise how plants need light.

4 Ask the children questions that will help them realise that, without the sun, we would not have warmth, light, plants, life. Say a big 'thank you' to God for making the sun.

Where does the sun go at night?
It is always daytime somewhere! And God is always with everyone.

 Make sure the paint is the consistency of cream, so that it does not dribble. If possible, place pictures flat to dry when finished.

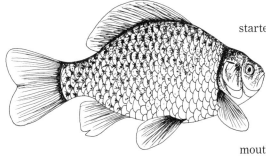

1 Tell the story of Jonah not listening to God (Jonah 1,2). Explain that he was swallowed by a giant fish and later coughed up on to dry land. He then went and told the people about God (Jonah 3).

2 Discuss what it would be like to be inside a fish! Chat about how Jonah

started singing to God inside the big fish: no matter where we are, God is still with us.

3 Examine a real fish (or picture) closely, noticing details such as the shape of its body, scales, the position of its fins, eyes, mouth, and so on.

4 Encourage the children to paint their own fish.

5 Afterwards, describe any details in their paintings you see. Particularly use words like 'scales' to protect his body, 'fins' and 'tail' to help the fish go the way he wants, 'gills' to breathe, 'eyes', 'mouth'.

6 Remind the children that Jonah started singing to remind himself that God still cared. Ask: 'What helps you remember that God cares?'

 Have a small cut-out of 'Jonah' that each child can glue onto their painting when it is dry.

Do you think Jonah liked it inside the big fish?
Where do you not like to be?

Painting with fingers

Finger-painting is great fun and a 'no threat' activity. Young children find it easier to paint using their own fingers than trying to hold a brush. If they create something they do not like, it is so easy to start again. (Show them how to use the flat palm of a hand to literally 'wipe the slate clean'.)

Finger-painting is an excellent pre-writing activity. These activities help gain control of large arm movements, right down to fine hand control. For slightly older children, guided finger-painting activities also help them to follow directions (another important skill).

Always make sure you use plastic aprons and work in an easy-clean area. You will need water for washing and towels, with at least one adult assistant to help clean painty hands. Because of its messy nature, it is better to work with six or fewer children at a time.

Get the children to work standing up, with enough table space to work freely. Often finger-painting is done on a plastic surface. You could use a tray or put the paint directly on to a wipeable and waterproof surface. Put a dollop of paint at each place on the table and let the children enjoy 'drawing' in it.

Alternatively, get the children to dip their fingers into the paint, and then smudge in onto a sheet of paper. Finger-painting onto paper can also be used to make finger or thumb prints join together to make a host of different creations: butterflies, caterpillars, ants and people. Use fine marker pens to add on ears, eyes, legs, and so on, once the paint has dried. Painting the events of a Bible story and recreating the various scenes with finger-paints, will absorb a child's attention and bring them into close contact and involvement with what happened. Finger-painting adds an active dimension to storytelling and story-listening.

God feeds his people

Manna in the morning
Exodus 16; 17:1–7

10 mins

You will need:
crayons, orange or brown paint in small plastic containers, paper, a plastic-covered table, cover-up and clean-up equipment

Jeremiah sees a potter

Patterns and shapes
Jeremiah 18:1–12

15–20 mins

You will need:
a real pot with a geometric design or pattern, brightly coloured paints in small plastic containers, a sheet of paper per child with a 'pot' outline drawn on, cover-up and clean-up equipment

The lost sheep

Painting a Bible story
Luke 15:1–7

5–10 mins

You will need:
green paint, cover-up and clean-up equipment, trays (optional)

God looks after us like the good shepherd looked after his sheep.

How do you know God cares about you?

1 Tell the story of God providing manna for the Hebrew people to eat when they were living in the desert.

2 Encourage the children to draw the people in the desert on paper.

3 Put on aprons and take the pictures to the painting table. Gather a small group of children around the table and show them how to put their finger into the paint and then onto the paper to create a piece of 'manna'. Talk about how God looked after his people and gave them food to eat.

4 Encourage the children to make spots of 'manna' on their own pictures.

5 When the children have finished, put the pictures somewhere to dry. (Keep the finger paint fairly thin, so that it will dry quickly.)

 Warn parents and carers beforehand to let children wear 'working clothes' for this session. Occasionally a child will not want to get their hands dirty. We can encourage – but always respect the child's wish. Allow them to use crayons, instead, to draw the manna.

The manna was suddenly there in the morning – God sent it for the people.

How does God look after you?

---

1 Tell the story of Jeremiah watching the potter: 'One day Jeremiah went to watch a potter making pots. The potter kept shaping and changing his clay until he made a lovely pot. Jeremiah thought, That's what God is like.'

2 Show the children the pot you have brought and discuss its design. Then put the pot away so that the children do not copy its design.

3 Talk about how God has made us like him. God can make things and we can make things too.

4 Show the children how to dip their finger into the paint and then 'draw' simple circles, triangles, lines, and so on, on the pot outline to create a pattern.

5 When these are dry, display them for everyone to admire.

 Warn parents and carers beforehand to let children wear 'working clothes' for this session.

God is called the 'Creator' because he can make things. What can you make?

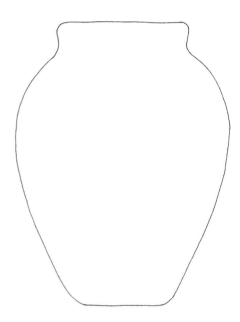

---

1 Before you start, cover the table with plastic or set out trays. Pour green paint on each tray or at each space around the table.

2 As you tell the story, draw directly in the paint. Let the children copy you in theirs.

(Smooth out the paint with one hand to create a 'field'.)

A farmer had lots of sheep.

(Draw wobbly circles with 'legs'.)

The sheep had curly wool all over them.

(Smooth out the paint; draw curls and spirals.)

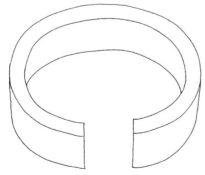

The shepherd looked at the big mountains.

(Smooth out the paint; draw a zigzag horizon.)

Up the sheep went, eating the sweet green grass.

(Draw a path winding upwards.)

Then the shepherd said, 'Home time. Down we go.'

(Retrace the path.)

The shepherd had a special place where he kept the sheep safe at night. He counted all the sheep as they walked in.

(Draw a simple sheep pen, with an opening in one side.)

Uh-oh! One sheep was missing. The shepherd climbed back up the mountain. He looked this way and that.

(Move your finger around.)

He found his missing sheep. Hooray! He carried it gently back to the others.

(Draw the route back to the sheep pen.)

The shepherd really loved his sheep. He was so happy he had found her again.

 Use this method to illustrate other Bible stories, using simple lines and shapes.

Painting using other techniques

There are many ways to create exciting results with paint, often combining with other art activities, such as drawing.

- Use drinking straws to blow very runny paint on a sheet of paper. This is a great way to create interesting plants, trees or part of an underwater scene – the possibilities are endless!

- Sponge painting can be used to create stones, feathers on a bird, grassy effects or texture on boats.

- Blow bubbles into a mixture of thin paint mixed with washing-up liquid, and then gently lower a sheet of paper so that it just touches the bubbles. This gives a lovely circular all-over pattern which is great for watery or cloudy effects. When it is dry, enhance this with a second complementary colour of bubbles.

- Create different textures by adding different substances to the paint. Try mixing some sand into the yellow for a desert scene. Salt gives an interesting shine when the paint is dry.

- Put a little food essence into paints to stimulate the sense of smell: lemon in yellow, vanilla or chocolate in brown, strawberry in red, peppermint in green or blue.

What we paint with also generates interest. Try using a feather, a piece of sponge with a clothes peg for a handle, an old squashy balloon that can be pressed against the paper, or a very large house-painting brush on extra large paper.

Paint on different colour paper (white or yellow paint on black or purple paper to create a night sky, for example).

Remember that the pleasure comes from the children learning to mix paints themselves. If this is daunting, get an art book that explains colour-mixing and do some experimenting yourself. First, introduce the children to mixing two colours together, such as red and yellow: see how many shades of orange they can make on a sun picture. Children experience the joy of creation when they see new colours appearing. Next, try mixing different shades of blue by adding white and very little yellow, which can make interesting water scenes.

Jesus walks on water

Painting with marbles
Mark 6:45–52

You will need:
sample sheet of rolled marble paper and a small drawing of Jesus; marbles; blue, purple, sea green and white paint (the consistency of cream) in shallow bowls; large baking trays (one per child); spoons; pale blue paper that will fit into the trays; cover-up and clean-up equipment; A4 sheets of blank paper; spoon

Hidden treasure

Comb painting
Matthew 13:44

You will need:
small sheets of heavyweight plastic (or trays), sheets of plain paper, brown and yellow paint, broad-toothed combs, shiny collage scraps, glue, cover-up and clean-up equipment

The story of the seeds

Batik, without wax
Mark 4:1–9

You will need:
plastic squeezy bottles with nozzles (one per child), flour, salt and water mixture, a large piece of white fabric (for example, a piece of sheeting), brushes, fabric paint, flour sieve, jug, cover-up and clean-up equipment

*this time is spread across 3 sessions

1 Show the children your marble paper sample. Demonstrate the process: put a sheet of paper flat in the baking tray. Put a marble into the paint. Pick up the marble with a spoon and drop it gently onto the paper in the tray. Tilt the tray around, so that marble rolls over the paper, distributing paint as it goes. Repeat this process, using different colours if you wish, until the paper is filled.

2 Help the children to make their own patterned sheets.

3 While the sheets are drying, tell the story of Jesus walking on the water. Use your prepared paper as the 'sea' and a picture of Jesus to illustrate what you are saying.

4 Suggest the children draw their own pictures of Jesus so that they can tell the story again at home.

5 Think about how special Jesus is: he can even walk on water!

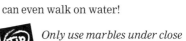 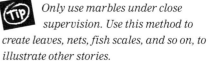 *Only use marbles under close supervision. Use this method to create leaves, nets, fish scales, and so on, to illustrate other stories.*

> What do you think would happen if you tried to walk on water?
>
> Why is Jesus so amazing that he can walk on water?
>
> What other amazing things did he do?

---

1 Demonstrate the process. Put a small dollop of paint on a plastic surface. Use a comb, in wavy motion, to spread the paint. Talk about making 'furrows' on the 'field'. Carefully place a sheet of paper over the paint; press down lightly; then peel the paper off to reveal a print. Leave this to dry.

2 Encourage the children to make their own 'fields'. While these are drying, tell Jesus' story of the hidden treasure, from Matthew 13:44.

3 If you have time, let the children glue shiny scraps, glitter and sequins on their field. Ask: 'What does your treasure look like? Does it look rich and important?'

4 Talk about what is really valuable and important. Say that Jesus' story shows that following God is the most important thing of all. Tell the children that you believe this, too!

> What is really important to you?

---

1 This activity will take three sessions to complete, but the results can be spectacular!

2 Beforehand, mix equal quantities of flour and salt together with water to make a thin cream (it needs to flow freely but not too fast). Strain the mixture through the sieve to remove any lumps and fill the squeezy bottles with it.

3 Tell the story of the seeds, from Mark 4:1–9, using visual aids. Encourage the children to use their squeezy bottles to 'draw' features from the story onto the sheet: seeds, rough ground, thorny plants, birds, healthy plants. As they work, talk about how God is the one who makes things grow and who provides everything we need.

4 Encourage the children to fill the whole cloth with their floury-paint pictures. Leave the picture to dry, until your next session.

5 Next time, let the children paint over the entire sheet, with a medley of bright fabric paints. Again, leave it to dry until your next session.

6 Finally, let the children peel off the flour mixture with their fingers, revealing their original design, showing white against a colourful painted background.

> Make up your own 'thank you' song to God for the rain and sun that help the plants to grow.

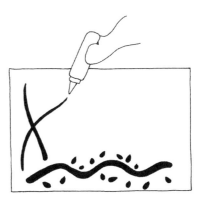

Paper chains

Paper chains are traditionally a decoration used especially at Christmas. There are lots of occasions when making paper chains can be used either as an effective way of storytelling, doing drama, or including everybody in a worship activity.

If you are making a paper chain with a small group of children, you will need one adult to supervise six children. If you are making a very long paper chain within a festival service for young children and their families, for instance at Christmas or Harvest, you will need additional help from parents to make, support and hang the chain, so that it does not tear.

● Paper chains are made from strips of coloured or metallic paper. The first strip is made into a circle, securing the join with glue or tape. A second strip is then threaded through and glued to make another link. Links are added until the chain is the required length.

● Packs of strips to make paper chains can be bought from stationers and departmental stores, but, although they are self-adhesive and therefore easier to assemble, they are expensive and, if you plan to use the strips for writing words on the back, you will discover some types are not suitable because the backing is black or glossy.

● The cheapest method is to make your own strips by guillotining coloured sheets of A4 copier paper. If you are working with a small group of children, use glue or tape to secure the ends. If you are using the activity in a service with lots of children and adults, you may find it easier to put a strip of double-sided tape on the end of each link. (Provide a bin for the bits!)

● Paper chains can be used to show visually how the Christian church is a family joined together by their love of God the Father, or is a group of people living in the way Jesus taught them. By inviting children to add a strip to the chain, they are being given an opportunity to show that they too, are part of that family.

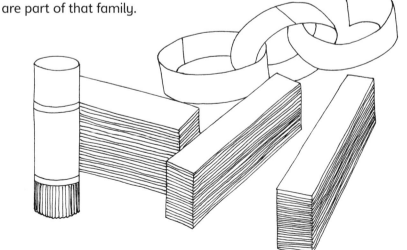

Helping Jesus

A paper chain to make as you tell a story
Matthew 4:18–22;
Matthew 10:1–4

You will need:
strips of coloured paper, with one larger or distinctive coloured paper strip

Paul and Silas

Prison chains
Acts 16:23–40

You will need:
ready-made paper chains or paper strips, glue or tape

The early church

Caring for each other
Acts 4:32–37; 9:32–43

You will need:
strips of paper (long and wide enough for writing and drawing), glue

1 Take 12 strips and write the name of a friend of Jesus on each one. (The list of names can be found in Matthew 10:1–4.) You could do this beforehand to save time. Write 'Jesus' on the larger or more distinctive strip, then make it into a circle. Explain that Jesus needed special friends to help him tell everybody about God, and to heal people.

2 Read the story of Jesus choosing four fishermen to help him from Matthew 4:18–22. As each name is mentioned, give that strip to a child to add onto the chain. Then add the names of the other friends of Jesus. You could make one long chain or have several small ones attached to the main link.

3 Chat about the kind of people Jesus chose to be his friends: fishermen, a tax collector, older people.

4 Ask the children who they think Jesus wants to be his friends now. Give everyone a paper strip. Help them write their name or draw a picture of themselves on it.

5 Join each strip onto the main chain to show that we can all be Jesus' friends.

Join your link to the chain to show that you want to be Jesus' friend too.

---

1 Before the session make some lengths of paper chain to illustrate the story.

2 Explain that a long time ago, when people were in prison, strong metal chains were used to fasten their arms and legs so that they could not escape. Choose two volunteers (or leaders or toys) to be fastened to chairs with the paper chains. The children will enjoy helping you, especially if they are tying up the grown-ups! Let each of them have a turn at being jailers.

3 Ask the prisoners what they feel like. Can they move their arms and legs? Could they escape without the jailers seeing them?

4 Tell the story of Paul and Silas, acting out the events, with singing and sound effects. When you reach the part about the chains falling off, let the children help to tear the paper chains so that the 'prisoners' are free. Chat about how the prisoners feel now. Say: 'Paul and Silas did not take the chains off. The jailer did not take the chains off. So who did?'

We can tear paper chains easily. But who was strong enough to break the strong, metal chains and set Paul and Silas free?

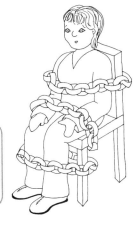

---

1 Say: 'Jesus' family was growing and growing. All the time, whenever people heard Peter and his friends talk about Jesus, or they saw ill people being healed, they thought, "We'd like to become friends of Jesus." So they did.' Encourage the children to draw lots of stick people or smiley faces on paper strips and put them together to make links on the chain.

2 Say: 'Friends of Jesus shared their money, homes and food. They looked after each other.' Get everyone to draw more people and faces, and join them onto the main chain.

3 Ask: 'What did Dorcas to do help people?' Help the children to add more links to represent her and all the people she helped.

4 Say: 'When people in Jesus' family (such as Aeneas and Dorcas) were ill, what did people do to help them?' Say that they prayed and asked Jesus to make them well again. Add more links for the pray-ers.

5 Explain that we can pray for people too. Give out more strips of paper. Ask everyone to draw a picture of themselves and, if they wish, someone they would like to tell about Jesus.

6 Join all these strips to make a chain. Then join both paper chains together and make into a circle to show how Jesus' friends are one family, loving and caring for each other.

How many people do you know in Jesus' family?
Tell Jesus about them now.

Paper folding

The art of paper folding or 'origami' sounds very complicated. It is often associated with very intricate, complex models. However, there are some very simple and effective ways of folding paper that even young children can manage.

These activities use a minimum of equipment and so need little preparation, although you might like to practise them beforehand. They are also clean and not messy!

Allow plenty of time for this type of activity. Demonstrate clearly, step-by-step, and repeat if you need to. Give the children plenty of encouragement to do as much of the folding as they can themselves.

Jesus' cross

Folding and tearing
Luke 23:26 – 24:12

5 mins

You will need:
sheets of A4 paper

The great feast

Party hats
Luke 14:15–24

10 mins

You will need:
large rectangular sheets of paper (A2 or flip chart paper), bright collage scraps, glue, crayons, scissors, a stapler, simple party food such as a drink and biscuit (be aware of any allergies)

Jesus walks on water

Folding and floating
Mark 6:45–52

10 mins

You will need:
sheets of paper about 20 cm^2, scissors, crayons, a bowl of water

1 Give each child a sheet of A4 paper. Get everyone to orientate their sheet into a portrait position. Show them how to fold down the top left-hand corner to meet the right-hand edge of the paper and make a firm, neat fold.

2 Next, get everyone to fold the top point of the triangle (or the top right hand corner) across to the bottom-left point.

3 Help the children to fold the paper in half lengthways twice.

4 Encourage everyone to tear their paper in half lengthways, starting at the square end.

5 Let the children unfold the paper and enjoy their surprise when they find it has made a cross.

6 Talk about the shape they have made: where they have seen it and why it is important.

7 End on a positive note. Say that Jesus died on the cross, but he came alive again!

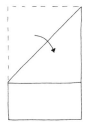 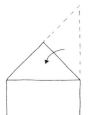    

Can you decorate your cross?

You could use your cross as a bookmark.

---

1 Tell the children that they are going to make party hats.

2 Give each child a sheet of paper. Help them to fold it in half. Next get everyone to fold it in half again and then open it out once. Then, with the crease at the top and the open end at the bottom, help everyone to fold the top two corners to meet in the middle. Finally, encourage everyone to fold up the bottom flap on each side to make a triangular hat.

3 Let the children decorate their hats with crayons or collage scraps. You could staple the bottom corners of the hats to make them more rigid.

4 While the children make their hats, tell them a story that Jesus told: 'A man was getting ready for a big party. But, on the day of the party, none of his friends could come. The man felt very disappointed and sad. But then he thought, there are lots of people who are not my friends yet. Perhaps they will come to my party. So he went out and asked everyone he met to come to his party. Lots of people went and they all enjoyed it. God is planning a party and wants everyone to come. Do you want to go?'

5 Then have a small party together while wearing the party hats.

Do you want to go to God's party one day?

What do you like best about parties?

---

1 Give each child a square sheet of paper. Help them to fold each corner into the centre to make four triangles meeting in the middle. (Fold the sheet in half twice first to get a centre point.) Encourage everyone to open the flaps out and draw 12 faces on the inner square. Get everyone to fold the flaps shut and draw a person on one of the flaps with his feet towards the fold.

2 Tell the children this story: 'Jesus' friends (*Point to the 12 faces.*) went out in a boat. (*Put all the folded papers in the water.*) There was a big storm (*Make ripples with your hands, but don't sink the papers.*) and the friends were frightened. But Jesus came to them, walking on the water! (*Point to the person they've drawn on the flap. It should now be opened up to make Jesus vertical on the water.*) Jesus said, "Don't be frightened! It's me, Jesus!" He climbed into the boat with them and the storm stopped at once. His friends were amazed.'

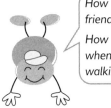

How do you think the friends felt in the storm?

How do you think they felt when they saw Jesus walking on the water?

 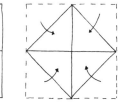

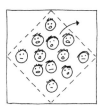 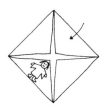

Papier mâché

Papier mâché literally means 'chewed paper', but that is a description of the way the paper looks rather than the way it is made! It is cheap and easy to make and produces very impressive results.

The process for making it can be very messy so make sure you cover all the surfaces – and the children's clothes! It is also a very tactile process, which can be quite therapeutic. Adult carers may enjoy working alongside the children and helping with the gluing.

To make papier mâché:

Dilute 'white' or 'school' glue 50:50 with water. (You could also use wallpaper paste or even flour and water paste but make sure it is non-toxic and does not contain fungicides.)

Tear the newspaper into strips about 2.5 cm wide. Dip the paper into the glue and squeeze off any excess between your finger and thumb. Lay the paper strips onto the base.

Work on one layer at a time. Ideally, allow one layer to dry before putting on the next layer. Working with small children at home this would be possible. In a large group setting, split the activity over two sessions. Complete the papier mâché in the first session and leave it to dry for at least 24 hours. Decorate the product in the second session.

You could have several children working together on one product or let a few children have a turn and then pass it on to another few. This not only encourages cooperation, but also keeps the children's interest during the long gluing process.

Papier mâché uses old scraps of newspaper and glue to make a beautiful finished product. In the same way, God uses us – with all our faults – and makes us beautiful. It is a process that takes time and requires us to be as mouldable as the papier mâché!

Philip in the desert

Desert scene
Acts 8:16–40

15+15* mins

You will need:
a large square piece of strong cardboard or wood, newspaper, glue for papier mâché, sand, paint, play people, cover-up and clean-up equipment
*15 minutes to make, plus drying time; 15 minutes to paint, plus drying time

Keep Moses safe!

A paper basket
Exodus 2:1–10

15+10* mins

You will need:
a big balloon, newspaper, glue for papier mâché, petroleum jelly, paint, a doll (preferably male), cover-up and clean-up equipment

*15 minutes to make, plus drying time; 10 minutes to paint, plus drying time

Jeremiah down the well

Construct a well
Jeremiah 38:1–3

15+10* mins

You will need
a plastic bottle, a roll of cling film, strips of newspaper, glue for papier mâché, grey paint, a play person, string, cover-up and clean-up equipment

*15 minutes to make, plus drying time; 10 minutes to paint, plus drying time

1 Tell the children that you are going to create a desert scene. Scrunch up some sheets of newspaper and arrange it over the card or wood base to create a contoured effect. Screw up some newspaper tightly and curve it round to make a ring-shaped pool.

2 Encourage the children to use the glue and strips of newspaper to cover the scrunched-up sheets and board completely, with several layers. Smooth down the rough edges and fold the ends under the board.

3 When it is completely dry, help the children to paint the circular pool blue.

Who can you tell about Jesus?
God took Philip to the desert just at the right time.

Mix the sand with some yellowy-brown paint and ask some children to paint the rest of the landscape to look like a desert. Leave it to dry.

4 Say: 'One of Jesus' friends, Philip, met an African man in a desert. (*Talk about what a desert is and put two play people in*

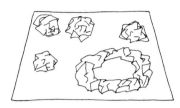

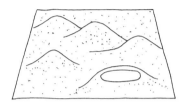

your landscape. You could just point to the desert if the paint is still wet.) Philip told him about Jesus and the man became a friend of Jesus. Philip baptised him straightaway in some water'. (*Put the play people in the pool or point to it.*)

 You can use your desert landscape to tell other stories from the Bible.

---

1 Say that you are going to make a big basket. Blow up the balloon and tie a knot at the end.

2 Help the children to glue several layers of newspaper over the bottom of the balloon to make a bowl shape.

3 Once the outer surface is dry, burst the balloon and let the inside dry out completely. Trim the edges and get the children to paint it yellow or brown. Let the paint dry.

4 Say: 'A long time ago the king of Egypt wanted to get rid of all the baby boys. One woman wanted to keep her baby safe. So

she put him in a basket like this one. (*Put the doll in the basket.*) She hid the basket among the reeds of the river. The baby was safe in his dry basket-boat. Then, the king's daughter found him. She took him out of the basket. (*Lift the doll out.*) She did not want to hurt him. She wanted to look after the baby. So God kept baby Moses safe.'

 Grease the balloon first with petroleum jelly to stop the papier mâché sticking. Hang the balloon from some string to dry, or stand it upside down in a cup.

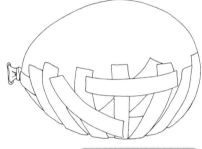

How did God look after Moses?
How did your mum or dad keep you safe when you were a baby?

---

1 Tell the children that you are going to make a well. Cover a plastic bottle, including the bottom, with cling film.

2 Encourage the children to put several layers of papier mâché (newspaper and glue) on to the bottle.

3 Let the outside dry. Then ease the bottle and cling film from the papier mâché and let the inside dry. Help the children to paint it grey at your next session.

4 Using the play person as Jeremiah, tell the Bible story. Say: 'Jeremiah talked to the people about God. He told them what God wanted to say to them. But the people

How did God help Jeremiah?
Can God help you in difficult times?

didn't want to hear, so they threw Jeremiah into a deep well. (*Put the play person in the well.*) But God was looking after Jeremiah. Some friends got some ropes and lowered them into the well. (*Put in the string.*) Jeremiah tied the ropes round himself and then his friends pulled him up. (*Help the play person out of the well.*) Now Jeremiah could carry on telling people about God.'

 Cut off the top of the bottle so you can turn it upside down and glue over the base more easily.

Printing with hands and feet

Printing with hands and feet is fun, but it is probably one of the messiest activities in this book! You will need lots of adult supervision, and plastic sheeting to protect the tables and floor. You will also need washing-up bowls and warm soapy water for washing afterwards, and towels for drying feet or hands – and anything else that has got painty!

Allow one child at a time to do the activity while everyone else watches. Ideally, you will need one adult to supervise the printing, one to supervise the washing of hands and feet afterwards, and another to write names on sheets of prints, and to top-up the paint trays as necessary.

When the completed prints are dry, you can:

• Leave the prints as they are a reminder of the ways in which we can use our hands and feet to help other people, just like Jesus did.

• Write on each set of prints, 'Thank you, God, for our hands (or feet)'. Use these words as a discussion starter about the difficulties those with disabilities may have. Take the sheet home to use as a prayer during the week. Link it with a story about a healing miracle.

• Use the prints to make a banner or poster. You could print everyone's feet in a line on one large sheet of paper and write on the words, 'Jesus said, "Follow me."' Alternatively, print each foot onto individual sheets of paper, cut them out and glue onto a background sheet.

• Be imaginative and use the prints as part of another piece of art. They could be the wings of birds or leaves on a tree. With felt-tip pens and a little imagination, fingerprints can be transformed into all kinds of faces and animals. Experiment and have fun!

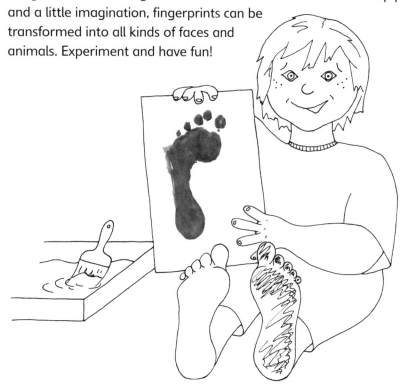

Jesus washes feet

Footprints
John 13:1–9,34,35

10–15* mins

You will need:
large sheets of paper, shallow tray(s), thick paint, protective sheeting and clothing, bowls of water for washing feet, soap, towels, parents and carers to help their own children (optional)

*depending on size of group

John baptises Jesus

Handprint doves
Matthew 3:13–17

10* mins

You will need:
birds' body shapes cut out from white card, white paint, sheets of light grey paper, a few white feathers, a shallow tray, thin elastic, sticky tape, a bowl, water, soap, a towel

*add drying time

God makes animals

Fingerprint caterpillar bookmarks
Genesis 1:20–31

8–10 mins

You will need:
a green ink pad (non-toxic), strips of white card 5 cm x 20 cm, joggle eyes or self-adhesive white dots, black felt-tip pens, a large magnifying glass, bowls of water and soap for washing, adhesive cellophane or laminator (optional), hole punch (optional), curling ribbon (optional)

1 Set up the trays with a small amount of paint in each. Ask everybody to take off their shoes and socks. Put them in a safe place.

2 Explain what you plan to do and assure the children that it will be fun. Help the first child put one foot into the paint tray and then onto a sheet of paper. Repeat with the other foot.

3 Guide the child to the washing area, for their parents or carers to wash and dry their feet and help them dress again. Repeat this process with each child.

4 Ask if the children like having their feet washed. Help them to imagine what it would feel like for Jesus to wash his friends' dirty feet after a long journey along a dusty road. Why did Jesus do it? How did his friends feel?

 Some children might not like the idea of putting their feet in sticky paint or having their feet washed afterwards. Explain that Peter, one of Jesus' friends, did not like Jesus washing his feet either! If they still do not want to take part, say that you understand. Instead, draw round their feet (socks, shoes and all!) on coloured paper, and cut out the shapes and glue them onto background paper.

Would you like Jesus to wash your feet?

What do you think it would feel like?

---

1 You will need one adult to supervise four to six children. Let one child at a time make the handprints while the others watch.

2 Help each child to press the palm of one hand into the tray of paint; then press down firmly, twice, onto a sheet of grey paper.

3 Leave the prints to dry while they wash their hands and clear up.

4 Cut out the handprints separately, leaving a narrow grey border. Attach the handprints (wings) onto the bird's 'body', one on each side (bird body template on page 82). Add a few feathers, if available. Help the children to draw on the eyes and a beak. Tape a length of elastic to the top of the back so that the children can hold the birds.

5 Talk about how a dove is a gentle and soft bird. Stroke the feathers and feel their softness. Explain that a dove is often used in the Bible as a picture of God's Holy Spirit coming to show God's love for Jesus and for each of us. Tell the story of Jesus' baptism and let the children 'fly' their doves at the appropriate point.

On the right is another way to make a dove from just one handprint.

 *Make several doves and hang them together to make a mobile. Watch as they gently move in the breeze.*

Have you seen a real dove? They make a soft noise like this: 'Cooo-cooo.' Can you make a sound like a dove?

1 Help each child to print a wiggly row of fingerprints along a strip of card to represent a caterpillar. They should print a thumbprint at one end. (Make sure everyone washes their hands immediately to remove the green ink.)

2 Encourage each child to draw legs and facial details on the caterpillar with a felt-tip pen. Use a wobbly eye or a self-adhesive white dot for the eye.

3 Chat about God making lots of different and interesting animals. Let each child tell you about their favourite animal and what makes it so special to them.

Did you know that the patterns on your thumbs and fingers are not the same as anybody else's? Only God could have had a wonderful idea like that!

4 You could cover each bookmark with adhesive cellophane or laminate it to make it last longer. You could punch a hole and add some curling ribbon to the end.

5 When the caterpillar bookmarks are completed, show the children how to look at their fingerprints and thumbprints through the magnifying glass. Suggest they look at their friends' fingerprints and see if any are exactly the same as theirs.

 Visit a butterfly farm or a museum and find out about real caterpillars. Enjoy finding out about their colour, variety and amazing life cycle.

Printing, with a variety of materials

Printing with objects is interesting and can be a lot of fun. The technique can be used for a variety of purposes, such as cards, wrapping paper, banners and posters. It provides an opportunity to be imaginative and creative. Using natural objects also helps the children to discover the variety of patterns and shapes in God's world. Here are some ideas to try:

- Print with vegetables and fruit. Apples and pears, cut in half, are effective because they show the pattern of the core. Slices and sticks of carrot, or potatoes cut into shapes, can be used to make patterns, abstract prints or pictures.

- Use leaves, bark and tree fruit, such as sycamore wings. Apply paint with a brush or roller to the back of leaves, where the veins are more prominent. Check that natural materials are reasonably dry, and choose leaves that are non-poisonous and do not contain a lot of sap.

- Interesting sponge shapes can be purchased from educational suppliers and craft shops. However, if you need simple, geometric shapes it is cheaper to cut your own blocks from household sponges. Other everyday items which can be used for printing are bubble wrap, netting, corks, string, corrugated card and plastic bottle tops.

Use thick paint, ideally ready-mixed acrylic. Put a little paint into shallow trays. Preferably use only one colour at a time so that the colours remain bright and not muddy-brown.

- To make cards and wrapping paper for special occasions, you may be able to borrow some stamp blocks and ink pads. These blocks are very effective but an expensive investment.

- Make your own printing blocks by gluing swirls of parcel string onto wooden blocks.

- Make banners using fabric paint applied with sponges and stencils. Put a sheet of cardboard under the fabric to absorb excess paint.

 If you are working on a group project it is better to take turns and have two children working on it at one time.

God makes plants

All kinds of leaves
Genesis 1:11–13

no limit

You will need:
a selection of leaves, up to four colours of paint, shallow containers, rollers and brushes, paper, hard fruit such as apple or pear, a knife (for adult use only), cover-up and clean-up equipment

David's song

Sponge-print sheep
Psalm 23

10 mins

You will need:
A4 sheets of green paper, sheep shapes cut from household sponge or a large potato, small sticks of potato or cardboard, white and black paint, felt-tip pens, cover-up and clean-up equipment

Jesus stops a storm

Boat on the sea
Matthew 8:23–27

15 mins

You will need:
bubble wrap; corrugated card; a piece of household sponge; A4 sheet of card or paper; blue, green, light grey and brown paints; shallow containers; a roller; cover-up and clean-up equipment

1 Protect surfaces and clothes. You will need adult supervision and it is best to work with a maximum of four children in each group.

2 Put a small quantity of thick paint into shallow containers. Restrict the colours to two containers per table.

3 Demonstrate how to apply paint onto the back of the leaves with a brush or small roller. Press the leaf onto a sheet of paper to make a print. Choose a variety of interesting leaf shapes. In the UK, try horse chestnut, sycamore, beech, rose and bracken leaves. Help the children to marvel at the variety of plants and trees God has made. Encourage the children to notice the different shapes and colours of leaves they have used for their leaf picture.

4 While the prints dry, say that you are going to show them something that no one has seen before! Cut an apple or pear in half horizontally and see the pattern inside. They are the first people to see it!

5 Count how many leaf prints you have made between you. If possible, look at a real tree: can you count the number of leaves that God has made on just one tree?!

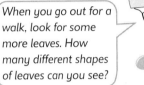

When you go out for a walk, look for some more leaves. How many different shapes of leaves can you see?

---

1 This activity will remind the children that God is like a shepherd.

2 Give each child a sheet of green paper and encourage them to print a sheep's body and head using the sponge shapes. Get them to print legs using sticks of potato or cardboard.

3 Say that David wrote a song about how God looked after him. 'God is like a shepherd looking after his sheep,' he sang. Talk about the kind of things the sheep would need and encourage the children to draw them onto their pictures:

a stream for water, lines to represent juicy grass; maybe a few flowers to make it a beautiful place to be and a tree for shade.

4 When the paint has dried sufficiently, get the children to draw eyes, ears and a mouth on each sheep's head.

5 Help everyone to write 'God cares for me' at the top of each picture as a reminder that God cares for all of us and provides us with everything we need – just like the shepherd cares for his sheep.

 Adapt this idea for other Bible stories about sheep, such as: The Lost Sheep (Luke 15:4–6), Jesus the Shepherd (John 10:11) and Ezekiel (Ezekiel 34:11–15).

Think of all the ways God cares for you.

---

1 Before the session cut a length of bubble wrap approximately 10 cm x 20 cm for each child. Shape the top as you would draw the sea (shown here). Cut out boat shapes from corrugated card, and cloud and sail shapes from sponge.

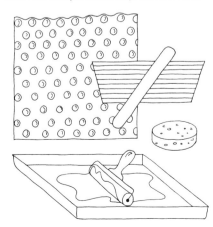

2 Give each child a piece of bubble wrap and a sheet of card. Help them to apply blue and green paint to the bubbly side of the bubble wrap, with a roller, so the two colours merge slightly. Encourage them to print this across their card to represent water. Comment that the sea looks lovely – just right to go for a ride in a boat!

3 Encourage the children to print a boat with sails and some clouds on their pictures using the templates.

4 Say: 'One evening, Jesus and his friends were sailing in a boat. A strong wind began to blow and the waves got bigger. The boat rocked from side to side. What do you think it would have been like in that small boat in a storm? Jesus' friends were scared. Then Jesus told the wind to be quiet and the waves to be still, and immediately they were. What do you think his friends said then? The sea was beautifully calm again, just right for sailing in a boat.'

5 Suggest that the children use their (dry) prints to re-enact the story.

Have you ever felt frightened during stormy or windy weather?

Ask Jesus to look after you.

Puppets

You can make puppets out of almost anything – cardboard rolls, seed pods, vegetables, paper bags, or odd socks! It is always a good idea to collect interesting junk because projects like puppets can utilise all sorts of odds and ends.

The ideas in this section will hopefully inspire you, but it is worth browsing through library books on puppetry to get other ideas. You may wish to put out a variety of scrap materials and let the children create a puppet. Have the materials ready and sorted in open, easily accessible containers, so that the children can take what they need. Include pairs of round-ended scissors, glue and paints. Think about the sort of puppet you are making and have only the suitable materials displayed. For instance, kings need shiny paper, gold buttons and velvet or patterned materials whereas donkeys need grey paint and black knitting wool. (If you use wool for hair or manes, cut suitable lengths before the session by wrapping it around your hand and then cutting through the loops.) Use containers such as plastic tubs or shoeboxes to label and store leftover materials for other projects.

The fun of puppets is not only in the making but also in using them. There is something about puppets that can cause children to lose their inhibitions. You may find that the shyest child suddenly becomes the big booming voice of Moses, for example. This opportunity to try out being other people is one of the most exciting aspects of puppetry. The realms of imagination open up new understandings of God's word to us.

You could make finger puppets by painting faces directly onto the children's fingers. Use small bits of cloth to wrap around for clothes. Alternatively, glue a paper shape onto a finger. Paper bag and paper plate puppets are easy to make and use, and are inexpensive.

 Remember, very young children can feel frightened by very big puppets, so opt for smaller 'friendly' varieties.

Mr Proud and Mr Sorry

'Talking' hand puppets
Luke 18:9–14

 10 mins

You will need:
face paints, hand-washing facilities, extra adult help

Be aware of skin conditions when drawing on children's hands.

Walking, leaping and praising God

A 'walking fingers' puppet
Acts 3:1–10

10–15 mins

You will need:
a prepared or finished puppet, a puppet shape with leg holes already cut out for each child, crayons or coloured paper, scraps to decorate, round-ended scissors

Jairus and his daughter

Puppets from pegs
Mark 5:35–43

 20–25 mins

You will need:
wooden 'dolly' clothes pegs with rounded ends (at least one per child), fine felt-tip pens (to draw faces), small squares of light-weight fabric (for clothes and headdresses), short lengths of knitting wool or ribbon (to tie fabric in place), white glue

1 Encourage the children to watch as you quickly paint a 'talking hand' shape onto your hand. (Have one already painted onto your dominant hand.)

2 Use your 'talking hand' puppets to tell the story, letting one talk for 'Mr Proud' and the other talk for 'Mr Sorry'. Say: 'Once there were two men: Mr Proud "Hello!", and Mr Sorry "Hello!". Mr Proud thought he was very important. He prayed: "Thank you, God, that I don't do bad things like the other people." But Mr Sorry prayed a different prayer. He prayed: "Sorry, God, that I have done wrong things. Please forgive me." Who do you think God was happy with? The one who said, "Sorry!"'

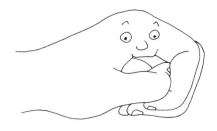

3 Invite the children to paint 'talking mouths' on their own hands. Have helpers available to give assistance, but be careful not to take over from the child.

4 Talk about how we all sometimes need to say sorry and that God is happy when we want to. Encourage the children to use their puppets to tell the Bible story to their parents and carers at home.

 *Give each puppet a distinctive voice. Practise lip-synch so the puppets' mouths open and shut in time with your words.*

Even grown-ups need to say 'Sorry!' sometimes.

God is happy when we say sorry if we have done something that makes him sad.

---

1 Start by asking the children to show you all the things they can do with their legs. Tell the story of Peter and John meeting the lame man and how Jesus healed him (Acts 3:1–10). Place your puppet in a 'sitting' position, with his 'legs' (your fingers) dangling uselessly. Then move his 'legs' to show him 'walking' and 'leaping'. Talk about how happy the man was that God had made his legs work again.

2 Invite the children to make their own 'walking' man. Give out the puppet shapes and encourage them to cut out and decorate them.

3 Encourage them to practise the story so that they will be able to tell their parents, carers and friends at home.

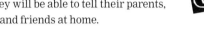
 For very young children, cut out puppet shapes beforehand.

Think of all the things you can you do with your legs.
Thank God for all the wonderful ways our bodies work.

---

1 Tell the story of Jairus' daughter, who was healed by Jesus (Mark 5:35–43).

2 Demonstrate how to draw a face on the rounded end of the peg. Encourage everyone to glue on clothes and a headdress. Help them to tie these on with wool, if necessary.

3 Encourage the children to use their puppets to help you act out the story. Negotiate with the children which puppet will be which character: you will need Jesus, the daughter, her mother, Jairus and the crowd.

4 After acting out the story, ask the children to speak for their characters, saying what that person might be thinking or feeling at the beginning and end of the story. By encouraging children's awareness of the thoughts and

feelings of other people, we are nurturing their sense of empathy. As they imagine the reaction of the different characters, their own faith is stimulated by the reality of how wonderful it is to experience Jesus' healing power.

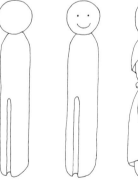 *Children are likely to want to re-enact this story repeatedly, so keep the props and puppets available.*

Who in the story do you think was most excited? Why?

What would you say to Jesus if he made you better?

More puppets

Simple puppets are easy to make, give children hours of fun and encourage them to use their God-given gift of imagination.

When children use puppets, they quickly take on that personality and Bible stories 'come alive' for them. Do not worry about having a formal script; children will happily ad lib and create their own dialogue.

Make a puppet theatre (see page 74) or improvise a stage. A table turned on its side, or a curtain attached across a doorway, will be adequate.

Make sure the actors can comfortably fit backstage and use the puppets. Other children can be the audience and then take turns. (It is helpful to mark a line on the floor that viewers must sit behind to watch comfortably.) Children's drama is impromptu and children will often launch into a puppet show, whilst others are still busy with other activities. Relax and let the children's play develop spontaneously! It is not necessary to have props. Again, children can happily imagine these. Keep the stage simple and uncluttered.

Encourage the children to use loud, clear voices that can be heard, and for each puppeteer to wait until the other has finished talking. Teach them that generally it is best if only the puppet who is speaking moves and the others keep still. This way the audience will know which puppet is speaking.

While children will gleefully use newly created puppets immediately, you can also build up a collection of puppets.

They are useful for children's play and are a great way to share a Bible story with them. As the children identify with the puppets, it helps them resonate with the Bible characters. At the same time, be aware that we are handling biblical truths here. We need to be exploring a Bible story to examine what could have happened, but not changing the story or altering its meaning.

David and Goliath

Paper-bag puppets
1 Samuel 17:12–50

15 mins

You will need:
'David' and 'Goliath' puppets prepared beforehand, one large and one small paper bag each (to fit on hands), paint, brushes, woollen strands, glue, aprons

A man by the road

Stick puppets
Luke 18:35–43

15–20 mins

You will need:
cardboard people shapes, crayons, drinking straws or bamboo canes, sticky tape

The kind traveller

A 'hobby-donkey'
Luke 10:30–37

15–20 mins

You will need:
a prepared donkey and man puppet, a stuffed or stick man, a narrow paper bag for each child, a pair of 'donkey ears' made from card for each child, a broomstick or bamboo cane (50 to 60 cm) for each child, sticky tape, marker pens, newspaper, glue, spreaders, short lengths of black wool, cover-up and clean-up equipment

1 Tell the story of David and Goliath (1 Samuel 17:12–50) in your own words using the paper bag puppets you have prepared.

2 Explain that, when we have courage, we can do something brave, even though we might feel afraid. Talk about how David was brave because he knew God was with him.

3 Give out the paper bags. Show the children how to make a 'Goliath' face on one, and a 'David' face on the other.

4 Leave the puppets that have wet paint to dry before using them!

5 Encourage the children to use their puppets together and at home to retell the story.

 In the Bible story, be careful not to make Goliath too frightening. Focus on David's courage and how he was brave because he knew God was with him.

 *When do you feel scared? You can always pray to God to help you be brave, even when you feel afraid.*

---

1 Stick puppets are easy to make and are one of the most versatile types of puppets. Simply tape a piece of thin bamboo or a drinking straw to the back of a cardboard person! Children find it easiest to hold the stick with the puppet at the top; but you can also tape the stick so that the puppet can be held from above or to the side.

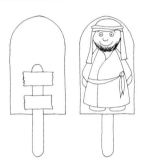

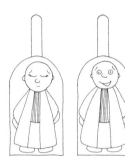

2 Before the session, make a puppet of Jesus and of the man who cannot see. Make the man who cannot see double sided – with eyes closed on one side and open on the other.

3 Tell the Bible story about the man who could not see Jesus – but who could still shout out to him (Luke 18:35–43)! Move the two puppets close together, with the 'eyes closed' side facing Jesus. Turn the puppet round as soon as Jesus says he is healed.

4 Help the children make their own pairs of puppets, so they can enjoy telling the story again at home.

 Stick puppets are ideal for using in a home-made puppet theatre. See page 74.

 *What would you like to ask Jesus? Tell him now!*

---

1 Tell the story of the kind traveller from Luke 10:30–37, using donkey and man puppets. Clip-clop along the road. Stop – look at the hurt man. Shake your donkey's head. Put the man on the donkey's back – sway as you carry him to safety. Clip-clop away.

2 Help the children to make a large donkey puppet. Help them to place one end of the broomstick into the paper bag. Then crumple newspaper into small balls and stuff these into the bag, until it is full. Tape the bag firmly closed, and tightly around the stick. Encourage the children to tape the ears onto the sides of the bag, and then draw the nostrils, mouth and eyes. Lastly, encourage everyone to glue on some wool for a mane.

3 Retell the story, encouraging the children to be the traveller, first riding, and then pretending to help the injured man as they walk alongside the donkey.

4 Encourage the children to empathise with the people in the story by chatting about what they might have been thinking and feeling.

 Bind the end of the broomstick with fabric so that it will not puncture the sides of the paper bag.

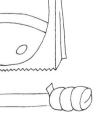 *'The kind traveller' is a story Jesus told. Why do you think he told this story? How can you help someone this week?*

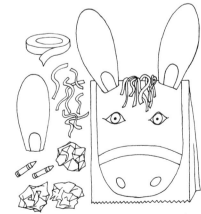

3 Puppet theatre

Illustrated here are two easy-to-make styles of theatre. Puppets are good for children because they encourage:

- imagination
- creativity
- improvisation
- language skills
- manual dexterity
- learning to take turns
- cooperation
- leadership
- story-planning, with a beginning, middle and end

Give your support, but try not to interfere. Young children do not spend time, as adults do, carefully planning out the detail. They tend to plunge into the activity, and the plot spontaneously unfolds as they go. For children, the process (what they do) is just as important as the product (the end result) in any form of creativity, including puppet plays. Of course, an appreciative and responsive audience is a great bonus. At the end of the show some little treat, like popcorn, for the puppeteers will be welcomed too! A simple puppet play might well develop into a project – setting out the 'auditorium' and theatre, making invitations, advertising leaflets and programmes.

Children of all ages love puppets. Watching them is great fun, and so is manipulating them. It is fascinating to watch a shy child disappear behind the puppet theatre and suddenly see a very animated puppet with a strong, loud voice appear. Puppets allow children to explore being someone else. Using puppets is a great way to build a child's confidence.

A table theatre

A table turned on its side makes a simple 'stage' for a puppet performance. Use sticky tape to add graphics to your stage!

Tiddlywinks theatre

Only the puppet who is talking should be moving.
Move other puppets to face the one who is talking.
Make sure the puppet can be seen.
Make sure the puppets always face the audience.
Keep your arms and hands out of sight.
Only have the puppets on stage that are part of the scene.

Alternative ways of using a cardboard box theatre

You can use any of three forms of access to the stage of your cardboard theatre depending on the most suitable angle for your venue. Ideally, the puppeteers should be concealed behind a curtain!

Rubbings

This is the process of taking a rubbing from an uneven surface.

Lay a sheet of thin, but strong paper over a textured surface and rub firmly with a wax crayon held sideways. Watch the pattern appear. If you use white paper, use dark or brightly coloured crayons. If you use black paper, metallic wax crayons or brass rubbing sticks are effective.

- It is possible to buy textured templates and animal stencils for children to use for rubbings, but it is cheaper and more effective to use natural materials. Stone, bark, leaves, and wood surfaces are all suitable, but check for splinters and sharp edges before using. Everyday materials, such as brick, concrete, netting, bubble wrap, embossed wallpaper and corrugated card work well too. Coins are interesting to rub because there are so many different designs. Use large ones that are easier for a young child to handle.

- Work in small groups with an adult supervising three or four children. If you do this activity outdoors, you will need extra supervision for safety.

- The children will need adult help to secure the paper over the item to be rubbed. Use masking tape over each corner. It does not matter if a child goes over the edges of the item to be rubbed as the design can be easily cut out and mounted on background paper. Smaller items, like coins, can be secured onto a table with Blu-tack.

- This activity provides an opportunity for children to explore the natural world through both sight and touch, and to wonder at its variety of shapes and textures. If you are learning about God creating plants and trees, go on a discovery walk and search together for suitable items to rub.

Zacchaeus meets Jesus

A tree to hide in
Luke 19:1–10

15+ mins

You will need:
large sheets of beige or yellow background paper, a large sheet of thin paper for rubbing, tree bark, leaves, brown and green wax crayons, card triangles and circles, glue, scissors, felt-tip pens

Building the walls

Brick rubbings
Nehemiah

15+ mins

You will need:
A4 sheets of thin paper for rubbing, grey or brown wax crayons, masking tape, either a length of lining paper and glue or empty small cereal boxes, tape

A missing coin

Coin headbands
Luke 15:8–10

12+ mins

You will need:
A2 sheets of brightly coloured or metallic card, sheets of white or black paper, large coins, silver wax crayons, Blu-tack, glue, tape

1 Get the children to take turns to rub either a piece of bark or an interesting piece of wood, placed under a large sheet of paper, with a brown crayon. (Check for splinters first.) Cut and shape the rubbing to represent a tree trunk and branches. Let the children help you to glue it onto the background paper.

2 Encourage everyone to make rubbings of lots of large leaves using green crayons. Cut out the leaves. Work together to assemble them at the top of the trunk to make leaves. Overlap the leaves and do not stick them all down completely.

3 Make a simple 'Zacchaeus' figure from a triangle of card with a circle for the

head. Say that he wanted to see Jesus but he was too short to see over the heads of lots of people, so he climbed into a tree. Hide 'Zacchaeus' in the leaves.

4 Make a similar, but taller figure for 'Jesus'. Place him by the tree. Tell the

story of how he invited Zacchaeus to come down, so that they could go to his house together. Chat about Jesus and Zacchaeus becoming friends.

 Make a larger picture and add a crowd of people, made in the same way as 'Zacchaeus' and 'Jesus'.

> Was Zacchaeus glad Jesus came to his house?
>
> Isn't it wonderful that Jesus wants to be our friend? How would you welcome Jesus?

---

1 Take the children outside to a safe area where there are bricks or concrete surfaces to rub. You will need additional adult help to ensure safety.

2 Tape a sheet of paper in place on the brick surface for each child. Show them how to rub with the wax crayons. Say that

> Nehemiah needed lots of people to help him rebuild the walls of Jerusalem. Can you work together to build a big wall (or picture)?

they will need to rub fairly carefully or the paper will tear.

3 Go indoors, and either:

Cut each child's rubbing into three brick shapes. Ask everybody to work together to assemble a wall collage using their bricks, just as Nehemiah encouraged the people of Jerusalem to help rebuild the city walls.

or:

Use the textured sheets of paper to cover cereal boxes and use these to represent the rebuilt wall.

4 Continually encourage and praise the children for their efforts, like Nehemiah encouraged his workers. When the wall is finished, sing a praise song to celebrate.

 Adapt this idea for other stories about building, such as 'The two builders' (Matthew 7:24–27).

---

1 This activity can be done with a group of four to six children at a time. Extra help would be useful for cutting out coins, and making each headband the correct size.

2 Cut the cards into strips, 4 to 5 cm deep, to be made into headbands.

3 Hold the coins on to a work surface with a small piece of Blu-tack and let the children make lots of rubbings. They will need ten each, but you could make some in advance if you think they will lose interest easily.

4 Cut out the 'coins' and give ten to each child along with a headband. Guide them to glue these onto their headband. Count aloud from 1 to 10 together, to make sure everyone has the correct number. Adjust

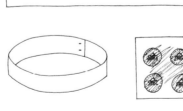

and fix the headbands so they are the correct size.

5 Talk about the woman in the story Jesus told. She was very sad when she lost one of her silver coins. What did she do? She looked everywhere till, at last, she found it again. She was so happy!

6 Count again to make sure everyone has ten coins on their headband.

7 Ask the children to sit quietly and think about how they feel. Remind them that God loves them and thinks they are very important people.

> Have you ever felt sad because you had lost one of your favourite toys? How did you feel when (if) you found it again?

Symmetrical shapes

In its simplest form, this technique involves taking a sheet of paper, folding it in half and opening it out flat again. Next, make a design with blobs of paint on one side of the paper. Then fold the paper back over, pressing firmly and opening it out to dry.

This method produces a picture that is perfectly symmetrical, like a mirror image.

It is ideal for even the youngest children, but you do need to use fairly thick paint and a reasonable quality paper for it to look effective.

● It is good to experiment with different combinations of colours, using two or three colours each time and different coloured paper for backgrounds. When the paper is pressed down firmly, the paint blobs will merge in places, giving a wider range of colours than the few used originally.

● Try using primary colours and let the children discover that, although they only put blobs of red, yellow and blue on their picture, somehow they now have orange, green, purple (and possibly brown) as well.

● This type of activity provides an opportunity for children to make discoveries about the colours in God's world and to wonder at the variety there is. It encourages them to think about shapes and patterning on creatures.

● Instead of an ordinary sheet of paper, you can cut out shapes of birds, fish and insects that are symmetrical and adapt this technique to create interesting creatures for pictures and mobiles.

● Try folding circles or squares of white paper into four, and tearing out pieces along the folds to make snowflakes. Like the real ones, they will all be different when finished. Laminate or sandwich between adhesive cellophane to make them durable.

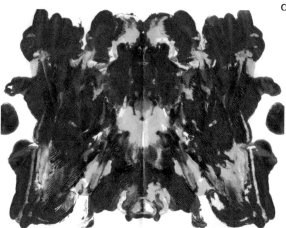

● Encourage further discovery by holding a mirror along the central fold of the artwork and moving it about to create more patterns.

The Day of Pentecost

A kite
Acts 2:1–4

10–15* mins

You will need:
sheets of strong paper; red, yellow and orange paint; curling ribbon; split bamboo cane; tissue or crêpe paper strips; cover-up and clean-up equipment; metallic gold paint (optional)

*add drying time

God cares for us

Making flowers
Matthew 6:25–34

10* mins

You will need:
simple flower shapes or circles cut from strong paper (several for each child); pink, purple and red paint; black or yellow tissue paper; glue; sheets of paper, plant sticks or green plastic straws; sticky tape; cover-up and clean-up equipment

*add drying time

God made... beetles!

Making mini-beast patterns
Genesis 1:24

10* mins

You will need:
A4 sheets of paper, paint, scissors, chenille wires, sticky tape, cover-up and clean-up equipment

*add drying time

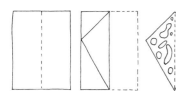 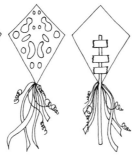

1 Cut out a rhombus shape from a sheet of paper, as shown, for each child. Hand these out and help everyone to fold it in half vertically. Show the children how to open the paper out and put blobs or swirls of paint on one side.

2 Encourage everyone to fold the kite back over, press firmly, and then open the paper again. Admire the way the paints have merged to create flame colours and how both sides mirror each other. Ask the children what these colours remind them of in the Pentecost story.

3 Tape lengths of tissue, crêpe paper or curling ribbon to the long point of the kite to make a tail. Fasten a cane to the back of the kite securely, so that it provides support.

4 Carry the kites outside and enjoy watching the tails moving in the breeze. Read or tell the Pentecost story from Acts 2:1–4, when the Holy Spirit appears like the sound of a strong wind and with bright flames.

5 Comment that we cannot see what is making the tails of the kites move but, because they are moving, we know the wind is there. In the same way, although we cannot see God, we can be sure he is here with us.

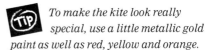 *To make the kite look really special, use a little metallic gold paint as well as red, yellow and orange.*

Look out of the window. Is it a windy day, today?

How can you tell?

---

1 Hand out the flowers or circles and get the children to fold them in half. Encourage the children to open them out and put blobs of paint on one side. Show them how to fold them again and press the two sides together firmly. Get everyone to open them up and admire the colours and patterns.

Which colour flowers do you like best?

How does God care for us?

2 Get each child to screw up a piece of tissue paper for the centre of each of their flowers. (This may stick with the wet paint; otherwise use a small blob of white glue.) Leave each child's flower to dry on a named sheet of paper.

3 Let the children clean up and wash their hands before sitting down to listen to the Bible story.

4 Say: 'Jesus talked about the flowers in the fields that he and his friends walked through. "Look, see how lovely they are!" he said. "Even great King Solomon did not have such beautiful clothes." Jesus said that, when we look at the flowers and see how God makes them beautiful and cares for them, we can remember how much God cares for us. We are worth much more than flowers!'

5 Fix a plant stick or straw to the back of each flower with tape. (Circles could be fringed round the edge to make petals.) Let the children take home their 'bouquet'.

 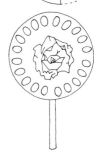

---

1 Did you know that a quarter of all known types of animal species are beetles, more than half a million? And naturalists think there could be 10 million still to be described! Children are usually fascinated by mini-beasts. This activity will encourage them to create some of their own.

2 Cut a paper oval for each child and help them to fold it down the long axis. Encourage the children to create symmetrical patterns by decorating one side of the paper, then folding it over. Get everyone to open out the folded paper and dab two spots of paint near one end, to be

eyes. If you want to make realistic lady-beetles ('ladybirds' or 'ladybugs'), put dabs of black paint on bright red paper.

3 When the creations are dry, tape three chenille wires across the reverse side, so that the ends stick out either side to form six legs. Bend these to make the beetle stand up.

4 Enthuse about the amazing variety, numbers, shapes and sizes of the animals God made when he made the world. Ask: 'What is the biggest animal you can think of?' 'What is the smallest?' Say that God made them all!

5 Adapt this activity to make other mini-beasts – butterflies made in this way are very effective.

God has made so many different animals of all shapes, sizes and colours!

What are you going to call your creature?

Templates, stencils and silhouettes

A template is a shape that you can draw round. Templates are useful for several of the activities in *Tiddlywinks: Make and Do*.

If you are not confident about your drawing skills, templates provide an easy option. The pictures on the following pages can be traced over or photocopied. Cut out the copies you have made and draw around them onto stiff card. Cut out and keep the card copies. They will be useful for the activities described and may be used for your own activities, too. When drawing around one template several times, experiment to fit as many as possible onto one sheet of paper. Sometimes it may be easier, and saves time, to cut through several layers of paper to produce multiple copies.

A stencil is like a template, except that the shape has been cut out, so you draw round the inside of the hole. Stencils can be created by cutting the desired shape out of some paper or card and painting over the 'hole'. You may need to use a craft knife with the paper placed on some cardboard or cork board to cut the shape accurately. Craft and DIY shops provide cheap, commercially produced examples. A quick and easy effect can be achieved by painting over the holes in a doily or Blu-tacking some shapes to paper and painting over them. Stencils can be used effectively to create repeated patterns, for example, stars.

A silhouette is an outline drawing filled in with black, a bit like a shadow. Silhouettes used to be very popular, especially for profiles. They require fine cutting skills and are best left to adults to produce. Silhouettes cut from dark paper and laid on a light background are very effective. You could try a black manger shape on a golden background or a black cross against a sunset.

Things to wear

Children love to dress up. Often simple items such as scarves, hats and pieces of fabric are as good as commercially produced dressing-up clothes, because they encourage the children to be more creative. Dressing-up helps children to develop their imaginative and empathic skills, as they pretend to be other people. Look out some old clothes and jewellery of your own or visit some charity shops to build up a collection.

Children enjoy making their own costumes and props too. Whether it is a hat, necklace, wristband, mask or badge, the fact that the child has made it, will make it more exciting and interesting.

Clothes and accessories can also be worn to make a point or a statement. One of the examples here will show you how to make a wristband as a memory aid and as a symbol of being a friend of God.

Whatever you make, ensure there are no sharp or pointed objects or edges. Cover the ends of staples with sticky tape so the points do not catch in the hair or to the skin.

The beautiful pearl

Pearl necklace
Matthew 13:45,46

 10 mins

You will need:
a pearl necklace (or picture of one), a circle of card 10 cm in diameter for each child, scissors, lengths of ribbon, a hole punch, crayons, adhesive cellophane or laminating pouches and a laminator

The rich man

Jewels and riches
Luke 18:18–30

 20* mins

You will need:
strips of card or paper, sticky tape, collage scraps, glitter, sequins or buttons, glue, pasta tubes, ready-mixed paint or spray paint, string, fabric, cover-up and clean-up equipment

*add drying time

Love and obey God

Wristband reminders
Deuteronomy 11:1,18–21

 5 mins

You will need:
paper strips 3 cm x 20 cm, crayons or felt-tip pens, sticky tape

1 Show the children the pearl necklace (or the picture). Talk about the beautiful, shining pearls and how precious they are. Tell the children that they are going to make their own pearl necklace.

2 Give out the card circles. Invite the children to make their 'pearl' as beautiful as possible. They might like to draw a picture of themselves on the circle or create a pattern.

3 Make the 'pearls' shine by covering them with cellophane or by laminating them.

4 Punch a hole in the top of the 'pearl' and thread a length of ribbon through to make a necklace.

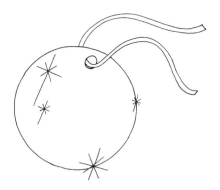

5 While the children make their necklaces, tell them the story of the rich merchant. Say: 'The rich merchant loved beautiful, expensive things. One day he saw a big, valuable pearl. It was the best thing he had ever seen. So he sold everything he had to buy it. Jesus told

this story to show that the best thing of all is being a friend of God. God's friendship is the most precious thing we can have.'

 Find out where real pearls come from.

> Why did the merchant want the pearl?
>
> How could you thank God for his friendship and love?

---

1 Tell the children that they are going to dress up as rich people. Take some suggestions about what they might wear.

2 Get them all to make fancy headbands. Give everyone a long strip of card. Invite them to decorate them with the collage scraps, glitter, sequins or buttons. Fasten the headbands around each child's head with sticky tape.

3 Encourage everyone to make a jewelled necklace. Give everyone a length of string and show them how to thread pasta tubes onto it. Tie the ends together. The pasta can then be painted.

4 When the children have made each item, encourage them to dress up in fabric cloaks, headbands and jewels.

5 Say: 'A rich man once came to Jesus to ask if he could be his friend. He was a good man but he liked being rich. Jesus said that, if the rich man really loved him, he would have to give away everything he had. (*Encourage the children to take off their cloaks, crowns and necklaces.*) But this was too hard for the man to do. He wanted to keep his nice clothes and jewels. They were more important to him than Jesus.'

> What stopped the man being Jesus' friend?
>
> Do you think he made the right choice?

 If you use spray paint, do it in a well-ventilated area, preferably outside.
You could thread jelly sweets onto the necklace instead.

Love God and do as he says

1 Before the session, prepare strips of paper with 'Love God and do what he says' written on one side. The template above is at approximately half size.

2 Give each child a strip of paper. Encourage everyone to decorate the plain side with the pens or crayons.

3 Wrap the finished bands loosely round the children's wrists and fasten with sticky tape.

4 Tell the children that God told his people to remember to love him and do what he says. God suggested that the

> Can you remember what the words on the band say?
>
> How else could you remember to love God?

people try lots of different ways to remember his words. One way was to 'tie them on their hands', a bit like having wristbands.

5 Shout together, 'Love God and do what he says' and raise your hand with the wristband into the air.

6 Suggest the children make another wristband for someone else. Then their friend can also be reminded to love God.

 You could also make a badge as a reminder to love God. Print the words, 'Love God and do what he says' on a small circle of card, and attach a safety pin to the back of it with sticky tape.

More things to wear

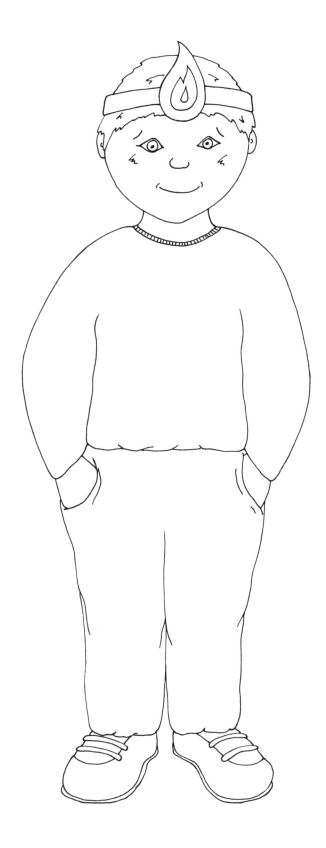

Faithful servants

Medals
Philippians 4:14;
2 Timothy 2:5

15 mins

You will need:
a card circle for each child, lengths of aluminium cooking foil, lengths of ribbon, a hole punch

The Day of Pentecost

Flame headbands
Acts 2

10 mins

You will need:
flame shapes cut from card; strips of card; sticky tape; tissue paper or paint in colours of red, yellow, orange and gold; glue; cover-up and clean-up equipment

Joseph in charge of Egypt

Egyptian clothes
Genesis 41

10 mins

You will need:
sheets of brown paper (40 cm x 20 cm for each child), long strips of bright coloured paper, scissors, crayons, sticky tape, glittery collage scraps, glue

Lydia

Tie and dye fabric
Acts 16:11–15

10* mins

You will need:
a white T-shirt or other white fabric for each child, rubber bands, purple cold water dye, plastic gloves, cover-up and clean-up facilities, area where items can drip without staining

*add the dying process to this prep time

1 Give each child a card circle and show them how to wrap a length of foil around it. Squash out any creases to make them look like flat, metal medals.

2 Use the hole punch to make a hole in the medal and thread a length of ribbon through it. Tie the ends together.

3 Talk about how people win medals when they have done very well in a sports competition. God wants us to work hard for him, as if we were running a race.

Then there will be a reward for us, a bit like a medal.

4 Have a ceremony when you award the medals to the children. As you put each

medal round the child's neck, say: 'I award this medal to (*child's name*) for their excellent achievement in…' (Try and award medals for a wide range of personal attributes, not only for skills and abilities.) Alternatively, you could just say, 'Well done, my good servant, (*name*)!' to each child.

> *What did you get your medal for?*
>
> *God is pleased when you work hard for him.*

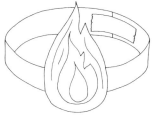

1 Say: 'Jesus had died and gone up to heaven. But before he went, he promised his friends a special helper would come.'

2 Give a flame shape to each child. Let them paint it in 'flame' colours or glue on pieces of tissue paper.

3 Encourage them to fasten the flames to the strip of card provided. Wrap this round each child's head and fasten with tape to make a headband.

4 Let the children wear their headbands when they are dry. Say: 'When Jesus' special helper came, he looked a bit like flames gently resting on everyone's head. Jesus' friends were filled with power to talk about Jesus in lots of different languages.'

5 Suggest that the children all try saying 'Praise the Lord!' in different languages: *Preist den Herrn!* (German), *Le Seigneur soit loué!* (French) or *Hallelujah!* (Hebrew)

> *Can you say anything in another language?*
>
> *What did the special helper help Jesus' friends to do?*

---

1 Before the session, prepare circles of brown paper. Fold each sheet in half lengthways. Cut out a semicircle from the side of the fold and cut a curve round the outer edge to make a shape like a rainbow. Open it out and cut a slit down one side of the fold so that it can fit round a neck.

2 Give them out and let the children decorate theirs with the collage scraps to make an important governor's collar.

3 Encourage the children to decorate a strip of coloured paper with a simple

geometric pattern. Fasten it round their heads with sticky tape.

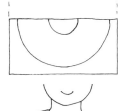

4 Say: 'A man called Joseph wore special Egyptian clothes like these. He had been in prison, but the king of Egypt gave him a special job to do and important clothes to wear. God looked after Joseph.'

> *How do you feel in your special clothes?*
>
> *Can you find out what Joseph's important job was?*

---

1 Give each child a T-shirt or piece of fabric. Show them how to bunch up areas of fabric and twist rubber bands on them. Explain that you are going to make the white fabric purple.

2 Get an adult to follow the dye instructions to dye the fabric while the children watch. Say that this reminds you of a woman in the Bible called Lydia. She sold purple cloth to people and was very rich.

3 When the process is complete, let the children remove the rubber bands and help hang up the purple fabric for drying.

4 Say: 'One day Paul and some other people met Lydia. They told her all about Jesus and she became a friend of Jesus, too.'

5 Remind the children that when they wear their purple T-shirts or look at their purple fabric, they can remember to tell their friends about Jesus, too.

> *Purple dye was very precious and expensive in Lydia's time.*
>
> *Who can you tell about Jesus?*

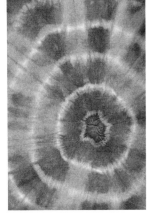

Wax-resist paintings

Wax-resist pictures can appear magical to children. They will be amazed to see the 'invisible' wax showing up under the paint. You could explain to them afterwards how the effect is achieved. Simply say that wax and water do not mix, so the watery paint runs off the wax.

It is worth practising this before showing the children, so that you get the right consistency of paint. The colour needs to be strong enough to show up, but watery enough to run off the wax. Use a good, thick wax crayon or candle.

Even very young children can get effective results. Allow them to make marks on the paper with the crayon and do their own paint wash afterwards.

This activity is one that stimulates a sense of wonder in young children. This is a time when, as leaders, we may need to ease back on our leading and organising, and allow the children to find their own words, pictures, and maybe movements and sounds, to explain how they have experienced and are experiencing God. Even when they understand the technique of painting over the wax, they will be fascinated by it, and may want to repeat it again and again. Encourage them and take this opportunity to listen to their spiritual responses. Give them time to talk and to reply in conversation. Be patient and wait for the words to come – sometimes they take a long time to surface.

The shepherds see angels

Make angels appear!
Luke 2:8–20

 5 mins

You will need:
sheets of white paper, white wax crayon or candle, watery paint (powder or ready-mixed) – dark blue or black, paint pots and large brushes, aprons, water, table coverings, clean-up equipment

A blind man sees Jesus

See what he saw!
John 9:1–12

 5 mins

You will need:
sheets of white paper, a white candle or wax crayon, paint wash (watery paint), cover-up and clean-up equipment

Promises to Abraham

Turning words into pictures
Genesis 12:1–9; 17

 10 mins

You will need:
sheets of white paper, a white candle or wax crayon, paint wash, cover-up and clean-up equipment

1 This can be a messy activity, so make sure you cover the tables, floor – and children! Have a bowl of water and paper towels available to clean up afterwards.

2 Before the session, draw the outline of an angel on the sheet(s) of paper with wax crayon, as thickly as possible. You could do one large one or individual ones for each child.

3 Sit with the children round the table. Show them the angel picture(s). The wax crayon should seem invisible on the white paper.

4 Tell the children that one night, some shepherds were sitting on a hill. They looked up at the sky and saw something amazing! What could it be?

5 Invite the children to paint the night sky with the watery paint. As they do so,

they will reveal the angel(s). What a surprise! Angels in the night sky! The angel(s) had some very special news for the shepherds.

 You could use another colour of paper as long as you use a matching colour wax crayon.

> *What was the news the angels told the shepherds?*
> *How do you think the shepherds felt to see the angels?*

---

1 Before the session, draw an outline of Jesus on a sheet of paper with the candle or crayon. It should be difficult to see.

2 Say: 'There was once a blind man, who had never seen anything. Perhaps everything looked like a white fog, like this sheet of paper. One day Jesus came along. He put some mud on the man's face and told him to wash it off in a pool. Suddenly the man could see for the first time! What do you think he saw?'

3 Paint over the wax picture to gradually reveal the picture of Jesus. How excited the man must have been to see! And one of the first people he saw was Jesus!

4 Let the children have a go at drawing Jesus with the crayon and painting over it. Alternatively, you could have some pictures of Jesus ready to paint over.

> *What would it be like if you could not see?*
> *How do you think the man felt when he could see?*

---

1 Before the session, use the candle to draw four simple pictures on separate sheets of paper. Draw a landscape, a tent home, a baby and a large family.

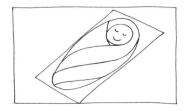

2 Say: 'God made lots of promises to Abraham. God promised Abraham a new land. (*Paint over the landscape picture.*) God also promised Abraham a new place

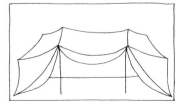

to live, a son and a large family. (*Paint over each of these pictures in turn.*) God kept his promises to Abraham. He keeps his promises to us, too. He is always good to us and promises to be with us always.'

3 Let the children draw themselves with the wax crayons. Encourage them to paint over these pictures and 'see' their self-portraits appear. Pray: 'Thank you, God, that you promise to be with us always.'

> *Can you remember God's promises to Abraham?*
> *What does God promise us?*

Weaving

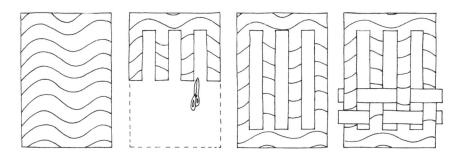

Most under 5s will find this activity quite difficult and they will certainly need one-to-one help. However, only part of your activity consists of actual weaving, and children will be delighted with the colourful result. As you work together, chat about God giving us fingers to do clever, delicate and fiddly things.

For simple weaving, use an A4 sheet of strong paper or thin card. Fold the card in half and cut from the fold to about 3 cm from the edge. You must have an even number of cuts, which will make an odd number of 'bars'. Cut off alternate bars, and then unfold the sheet, making a frame with wide gaps for the child to thread through their chosen materials. Cut lengths of paper, fabric strips, ribbon or thick wool in advance, making pieces longer than the width of the card. To finish, tape the ends onto the back and trim them.

- Do not worry about filling all the gaps. Even just three or four strips across will look colourful.

- Let a very young child be involved by choosing which strip to use next, even if an adult does the weaving.

- Having a colour theme will make the finished product look impressive, for instance you could use all pastels or different shades of blue.

- Use pages from flower catalogues or wrapping paper oddments to make brightly coloured strips – a good use for your leftover Christmas paper!

- If your children have enjoyed weaving, try it again soon, while they remember the technique.

Paul escapes

Paul in a basket
Acts 9:20–25

15–20 mins

You will need:
brown paper, scissors, corrugated card, brown wax crayons, a card person shape for each child, string, tape, Blu-tack

Paul makes new friends

A 'friends' mat
Acts 18:1–4

15–20 mins

You will need:
A4 sheets of card (or larger) for each child, strips of plain coloured paper, thick felt-tip pens

Lydia becomes a friend of Jesus

A wall hanging
Acts 16:11–15

15–20 mins

You will need:
a white A4 sheet of card for each child; crayons and felt-tip pens in shades of purple; purple strips of fabric, paper and ribbon; plastic strings ('scoubidous'); plastic drinking straws; tape

1 Cut each child a section of brown paper, about A4 in size. Shape the sides to make a basket. Demonstrate how to rub a pattern by putting the paper over the corrugated surface and using the side of the crayon.

2 Make these into weaving frames (see page 90). Give each child a person shape and challenge them to make it into Paul.

3 Help the children weave brown paper strips through the bars of the basket. Tape and trim them at the back. Fix a string handle to each basket.

4 Say: 'Paul had just come to know Jesus as his friend and now he wanted others to know about Jesus too. He talked about

Jesus to everyone. (*Move 'Paul' as if he is talking.*) Some people listened, but other people were cross and wanted to hurt him. "I will have to go away," Paul thought. But the gate out of the city was being watched all the time. "We will help you," said Paul's friends. They got a big basket and Paul climbed in. (*Blu-tack 'Paul' inside the basket.*) Then they lowered Paul down over the wall so he could run away. (*Try lowering the baskets to the ground, while holding the string.*) Paul went to a new place, but he still talked about Jesus there.'

Who helped Paul escape?

What would you tell people about Jesus?

---

1 Give each child a sheet of card and encourage them to decorate it. Cut the card to make weaving frames as shown on page 90.

2 Ask each child to name two or three of their friends. Write these several times along the strips of paper chosen by the child. Help them to weave these through the frame to make a mat. Tape and trim the ends of the strips.

Who do you think was Paul's very best friend?

Say thank you to God for your friends.

3 Admire all the mats. Talk about how good it is to have friends. Ask the children to sit carefully on their 'friends' mat while they listen to a story about Paul and some of his friends.

4 Say: 'Paul travelled around telling people about Jesus. When he needed money, he would work with strong woven material and make tents for people who travelled around, like him. Perhaps Paul sometimes made mats to sit on too! One day, when Paul arrived in a new city, he met a man called Aquila and found he was a tentmaker too. "Come and meet my wife, Priscilla," said Aquila. "Why don't you stay with us?" said Priscilla. "We can all make tents together. And we can all tell

people about Jesus, too." Paul stayed for sometime with Priscilla and Aquila. They were very good friends with each other and with Jesus, too!'

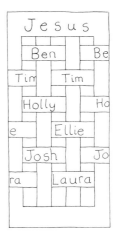

---

1 Tell the children about Lydia, who sold purple cloth: 'Only rich people bought purple cloth, so Lydia would have been quite an important person. One day, Lydia heard Paul talking about Jesus. Paul was saying that everyone can be a friend of Jesus. Lydia listened carefully. She decided that she wanted to be a friend of Jesus and for everyone in her house to love him, too. Paul and his friends came to stay at Lydia's house. She was so pleased that everyone can be friends with Jesus!'

2 Tell the children that you are going to do some purple weaving to remember Lydia's story. Give out the white sheets of card and let the children decorate theirs with purple patterns.

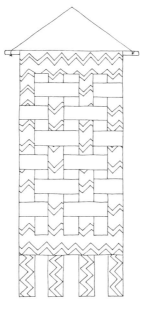

3 Make these into weaving frames and help the children to thread purple strips in and out of them. Tape the ends. Glue the cut-out bars along the bottom like a fringe.

4 Tape a drinking straw along the back edge, at the top. Thread a length of plastic string through the straw and tie the ends together to make a loop. Hang up the weaving to remember Lydia and that everyone can be a friend of Jesus.

What does your purple weaving remind you of?

What do you like about being a friend of Jesus?

4 Making a nativity scene

Make this project in four stages. These could be done during four separate sessions. Alternatively, it could be made during a half day session, interspersed with games, songs and other activities. If you have a large group of children, you could use a one-hour session and make all the elements in separate smaller groups, before building up the scene as the story is told.

Stage 1

You will need: dark blue backing paper, dark green paper, small silver stars, squares of white paper, glue

Use a large backing sheet of dark blue paper for the sky and a sheet of dark green paper for the hillside.

Stick some small silver stars in the sky.

Make several houses from squares of white paper with black windows and doors. Arrange them in an overlapping group in the background.

Tell the story: 'Bethlehem was only a small town, but it was very famous. King David had been born there many years ago and God had promised that someone even more important would be born there, too. Our story starts one night in Bethlehem long ago.'

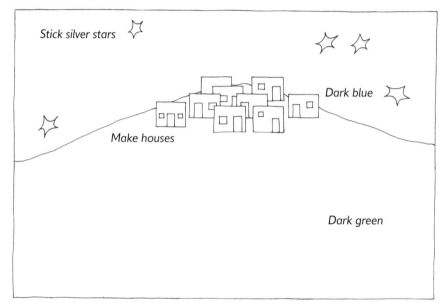

Stage 2

You will need: a box painted brown, sheets of paper or card, fabric, straw or shredded paper, small boxes or tubes

Make a stable from part of a box painted brown.

Draw or paint Mary, Joseph and baby Jesus in the manger on sheets of paper or card. Add details with fabric, straw or shredded paper.

Cut out the figures and glue onto small boxes or tubes to make them stand out from the background.

Tell the story: 'Mary and Joseph came to Bethlehem. Mary was tired because she was going to have a baby. The town was very busy and they could not find anywhere to stay. The only place was where the animals slept. Mary's baby was born and they put him in the animals' manger, where the hay was kept. But Mary and Joseph were happy because they knew their baby, Jesus, was the person God had promised.'

Stage 3

You will need: sheets of white paper, sparkly pens, glitter, stapler, glue, invisible thread, magazines, cotton wool, card, small twigs

Make angels from semicircles of white paper. Decorate these with sparkly pens and glitter. Use a stapler to make them into cones. Glue faces, cut from magazines, to the top of the cones. Hang the angels from invisible thread.

Make representations of sheep by gluing cotton wool onto cloud shapes.

Make the shepherds in the same way as Mary and Joseph (see Stage 2). Use small twigs for their crooks.

Tell the story: 'On the hills outside Bethlehem, shepherds were looking after their sheep. Suddenly an angel appeared. 'The shepherds were frightened but the angel told them not to be afraid.

He told them the good news about the baby. God's promised person had been born! Then lots of angels came and sang a song of praise to God. Afterwards the shepherds hurried to Bethlehem and found baby Jesus.'

Stage 4

You will need: a large glittery star, pretend jewels and shiny scraps of fabric, invisible thread, sheets of card

Hang a large glittery star from invisible thread over the manger.
Make the wise men from card like the other characters. (Include camels, if you wish.) Decorate their clothes with 'jewels' and shiny scraps of fabric.

Tell the story: 'Some wise men far away saw a new star in the sky. They knew it meant a king had been born, so they followed it all the way to Bethlehem. They took precious gifts with them and gave them to Jesus, the baby King.'

Index of Bible references

Index of story references

Have you enjoyed this book?

Then take a look at the other Big Books in the *Tiddlywinks* range.
Why not try them all?

The Big Orange Book
Themes: What's inside God's big book? All creatures great and small; Friends of God; Stories of Jesus
978 1 85999 716 1

The Big Red Book
Themes: Christmas is coming; People we meet; Stories Jesus told; God gives us food
978 1 85999 658 4

The Big Blue Book
Themes: All about me; God gives us... homes, clothes, food, etc; People who knew Jesus; Friends of God
978 1 85999 657 7

The Big Yellow Book
Themes: Easter; God gives us families; Friends of Jesus; What's the weather like?
978 1 85999 692 8

The Big Purple Book
Themes: Jesus love me; God love it when I... make music, sing, dance, look at books, I'm 'me'; Friends and followers; Materials and technology
978 1 85999 719 2

The Big Green Book
Themes: God's wonderful world; God gives us people; Let's find out about Jesus; God knows when I'm... happy, cross, sad, scared, busy
978 1 85999 695 9

'I love this! It's great!'
Sarah, leader of a 3 to 5s group in Victoria, Australia.

'...really pleased with your material and look forward to integratin Tiddlywinks into our existing programme.'
Marion, Scotland

Tiddlywinks Big Books are designed for use in any pre-school setting. The multi-purpose outlines are packed full of play, prayers, crafts, stories and rhymes; simply pick and mix ideas to meet the particular needs of your group. You'll find plenty of practical advice on setting up and running a pre-school group, plus ideas in every session to help you include adult carers. The children will love the illustrated activity pages.

A4, 96pp, £9.99 each

You can order these or any other *Tiddlywinks* resources from:

- Your local Christian bookstore
- Scripture Union Mail Order: Telephone 0845 0706 006
- Online: log on to **www.scriptureunion.org.uk/shop** to order securely from our online bookshop

Also now on sale!
Glitter and Glue. Say and Sing.
Even more craft and prayer ideas for use with under fives